THE LOCKDOWN BOOK OF ROTHERHAM'S CRIMINALS
(Book One)

Margaret Drinkall

Chris Drinkall

1

Introduction.

At the time of writing, Rotherham along with the other towns and cities of the world, is in a lockdown situation because of the Covid19 Virus. Unable to go outside apart from essentials, local people are confined to their houses and unable to continue with their everyday lives. Consequently as I am unable to do any research for any new books, my son Chris came up with the idea of reproducing again some of the many true crimes I have already written about. Rotherham has a long list of interesting local characters that have appeared in several of my local books and news paper articles.

The book is mainly aimed at new readers who have not read any of my books before, but as it contains new cases, I hope that it will appeal to the 'constant reader' also. Rotherham has always had more than its share of interesting characters such as Lady Barton, who kept a house of ill-repute and encouraged young 'artful dodgers' to bring her stolen goods. There was a couple called the Fritz's who managed to extract over £200 from the tradesmen of the town through their fraudulent activities. There is a highway robbery case which took place in the beautiful Wentworth Park. Where two elderly men were able to conceal £800 in the bottom of a dog cart as the two vicious criminals who attacked them, got away with a wallet containing tobacco.

All royalties for this book (and hopefully other 'Lockdown Criminals' books to follow) will be donated to the NHS for the sterling work they are doing during this worldwide crisis.

Enjoy and, whilst the crisis lasts, stay safe.

Margaret Drinkall
Chris Drinkall
May 2020

Contents

Chapter One: Rotherham Railway Riots.

The nineteenth century has often been embodied as the railway age. Vast amounts of railway tracks were laid all over the country and there was great rejoicing when it was known that the Sheffield and Rotherham Railway Company was to be formed in October 1838. The company would link the two towns and would hopefully bring prosperity to both. There were reservations however as the people of Rotherham thought that it would also bring the more disreputable elements from Sheffield to the town.

To complete this work many hundreds of men, called navvies were employed in laying down the tracks. The name came from the men who used to work on the canals, who were called navigators, but by the Victorian era it became a name for any manual labourers working on civil engineering projects. Hundreds of these men were employed by the Company and many were engaged working on the cuttings across Masbrough Common. It was said that the cuttings were so deep that work had to be undertaken all day and all night, by the light of several great fires.

So many workers were needed to complete the work that, Irish navvies were drafted into the town. In order to accommodate so many of them, temporary cottages and huts were erected on the Common and their families joined them and settled there. However the British navvies were not happy when the need for more men resulted in Irish men being employed. The relations between the two groups were never good at best, and when alcohol was involved in the scenario, violence was bound to ensue.

Trouble started in the Rotherham area when a rumour went around that the Irish labourers were undercutting English workers by working for 9d a day less. This was denied by the North Midland contractor Mr Stevenson, but the rumours grew to such an extent that fierce fighting broke out between the two groups. On Monday 8 October 1838 a group of these Irish navvies, taking advantage of the contractor's generosity, asked for an advance a sum of money from Mr Stephenson and spent it on ale. Many of these men lived with their families beside the tracks that were being laid at Swinton.

The row had started when an unnamed Irish navvy in a state of intoxication, had gone along the line and asked an Englishman for his pick axe. It was given to him and without any provocation he instantly struck the man in the back with it, injuring him badly. When the English contingent heard about this they demanded retribution, but his countrymen protected him and in retaliation the English refused to work with him. As a result he was driven from Swinton and quickly disappeared.

On Tuesday 9 October 1838 a vicious attack was carried out between the two factions and when the Rotherham police authorities heard about it, a group of special constables were quickly mustered to apprehend the Irishmen involved. At the same time a rumour went around the town that the Irish workers were making a determined effort to drive the English from the line at Swinton. Accordingly the English workers armed themselves with old scythes, hedging tools and anything that was available.

Word reached Mr Marsden, Mr Stephenson's agent and the men were stopped at Wath where the most dangerous weapons were taken from them. Mr Marsden spoke to the men and urged them to return to their work, but his words fell on deaf cars. It was reported that when the Irish men that were working lower down on the line, saw the English coming at them with weapons, they fled. At Rawmarsh about 100 of the English navvies met some of their Irish counterparts and they were severely beaten.

On Wednesday morning the English navvies mustered again in even greater numbers and in great patriotic fervour marched down the line towards Rotherham preceded by the Union Jack. There they drove away every Irish navvy they found at work on the line. Along the way they tore down any of the huts and mud hovels where the Irish families had made their home. The Irish also went towards the town of Rotherham, and at Masbrough they decided that they would retreat no more and would instead retaliate.

Tearing down a fence they made weapons out of the wood, others brandished spades and other tools of their trade. At that moment there was about 400 Irish navvies and around 600 English. By now word had reached Mr John Bland, the Chief Constable of Rotherham, that a riot was planned between the Irish and English workers. Some of the North Midland railway directors were busy surveying the line as the English approached, and the navvies were urged to go back to work offering inducements of an extra 1s per man. At Rotherham Mr Stephenson himself intent to stave off any rioting, spoke to the group of Irishmen and promised to protect them, if they would place themselves under his guidance.

He led them into the yard of the Sheffield and Rotherham railway station at Westgate, and there he gave them all refreshments which seemed to pacify some of them, although many still complained about their treatment. By now the news of the riot was leaking into the town centre and it was feared that if the riot at Masbrough broke out, the fighting men would retreat into the town and 'the streets of Rotherham would be one of carnage and devastation'. Within minutes, shopkeepers in the town centre hurriedly closed their premises, putting up shutters and locking their doors as they feared the fighting would lead to loss of goods and damage of property.

There was so much consternation among the inhabitants that two West Riding magistrates, Henry Walker Esq., of Clifton and Thomas Walker of Ravenfield were called out at 11.30 am. They had been instructed to take any measures 'to preserve the peace of the town'. In order to do this the magistrates called out the Rotherham troop of Yeomanry, a volunteer reserve who mustered in the Court House Yard to await instructions. The two magistrates also addressed the Irish contingent at the station yard, asking them to behave peaceably, or they would suffer the full might of the law. Then Henry and Thomas Walker, on horseback, went along the railway line until they met the English party and they urged them to disperse immediately and repeated the stern warning.

Eventually they too were induced to withdraw and it was almost 3.30 pm before the two magistrates returned back to Rotherham. Hoping that they had got the situation under control, they stood down the troop of Yeomanry with orders to be ready for duty at a moments notice. The Irish contingent were instructed to remain in Rotherham, as it was strongly felt that the battle would commence again once it became dark. The Irish navvies, safe in the security of the station yard were very uneasy because although they had been promised protection, they were aware that the cottages and huts at Swinton containing their wives and families were still very vulnerable and open to attack.

Between 5 pm and 6 pm Mr Stephenson returned back to Rotherham and reported to the two magistrates that he had been trying to placate the English navvies with some success, and many of them had dispersed. A strategy meeting was held with the magistrate Mr Henry Walker at the clerk to the magistrates office. It was then thought that if a riot took place, the Irish would be the stronger party, as by now many of the English had dispersed and he estimated that there was only about 50 or 60 remaining.

A decision was made to swear in a larger number of special constables and it was agreed with Mr Bland that these new 'specials' would be split into two parties. One would proceed with him to go to Swinton for the protection of the Irish families there. The other party under Detective Womack would patrol the streets of Rotherham during the night. Mr Stephenson told the Irish workers their plans for their protection and stated that they would receive 1s each to find beds for the night in Rotherham. He strongly urged them to stay away from the public houses 'and abstain from liquor' during their stay. It was noted later that the advice was taken and few people ventured out onto the streets, but the men in Rotherham were still very concerned for their families at Swinton. Meanwhile the inhabitants of Rotherham boarded up their windows and doors, as they hastily made preparations for the defence of the town.

When Mr Bland arrived at Swinton on the evening of Wednesday 10 October 1838 he found it all quiet as he and his party took shelter in one of the empty cottages. He sent patrols out during the night and at 5 am the next day the contractor Mr Stephenson arrived. He was anxious to find out the disposition of the English and to determine whether the Irish might be persuaded to return back to their work. At the usual hour when work would normally begin, he was pleased to find that many of the Englishmen preparing to return to work.

As he addressed them, he found that they still wanted the Irishmen off the site all together and they remained implacable towards them, promising to strike should they resume work. The Irish contingent were mostly still in Rotherham, but several men had returned back to Swinton under the cover of darkness to see their families in the huts. One of them had a wife who had just given birth the day before, and he had hoped to return clandestinely to assure himself of hers and the baby's safety. The small group had expected to get back to Rotherham before daybreak, but the English workers were up and about before they could return.

The small group of Irish found sanctuary in a cottage for a while and stayed for as long as they dared, but as more and more English assembled, they decided to make a run for it. Through surprise, they managed to get a good start and many escaped their pursuers, but those who were caught were cruelly beaten and would probably have been killed were it not for the interference of Mr Dodds. He was one of the Railway directors and was on his way to Rotherham when he saw the beatings, which he managed to break up. Meanwhile the remainder of the English, which numbered around 200-300 men, gathered together at Swinton and proceeded to swear vengeance on the Irish and on Mr Stephenson himself.

The men were still in a fighting mood as they swore that it was all his fault for hiring the Irish navvies in the first place and they vowed have his life and destroy his property. Mr Bland, who had been in the cottage at Swinton throughout the night saw what was happening, and feared the men would march into Rotherham again intent on violence. Courageously he approached one of the English men, who he suspected was one of the ringleaders and asked his name. In return the man took a swing at his head with a heavy bludgeon. Thankfully his arm was stopped by Mr Dodds or the result would have been fatal.

As it was, the blow landed on Mr Bland's shoulders and he was only slightly hurt. The Chief Constable then grabbed hold of the man and locked him up in a public house in Swinton. A group of Englishmen followed him and the prisoner, they swore that the man would not be taken and surrounded the pub. One of the specials was dispatched to Rotherham to communicated the state of affairs to the magistrates, and the men, suspecting that he had gone for the military, were determined to release the prisoner in order that he might make his escape before reinforcements returned.

They stoned the public house where he was being held and some of the special constables were hit. When the Englishmen tried to force their way inside, Mr Bland shouted to them that he was well provided with ammunition and anyone using force to take the prisoner must take the consequences. The men again demanded the release of the prisoner and they burst in through the door of the public house. The Chief Constable had no option but to release the man before returning to Rotherham to make his report. He had just reached the town, when another group of specials came from Swinton to inform him that the group of railway men were now being reinforced to an alarming extent by the potters of Swinton and some agricultural labourers.

9

This large groups of protesters were now marching along the line towards Rotherham, once again determined on ridding the town of the Irish. Mr Walker issued another order for the return of the Yeomanry which was taken to the barracks by a man on horseback. Another request was sent to the barracks at Sheffield asking that a contingent be sent to keep the peace. On hearing the news that another attack was imminent, Mr Stephenson sent the Irishmen who had remained in Rotherham, to Sheffield for their own safety. Several hundreds of them flocked into that town later in the afternoon.

At noon on Thursday 11 October a group of about a thousand Englishmen armed with 'a variety of vicious weapons' crossed the meadows and the river at Ickles. They then approached Masbrough, but not finding any Irishmen at work they proceeded into the town centre. They got as far as the Sheffield Road and were proceeded along Westgate, where a party of them were threatening to pull down Mr Stephenson's house. However it seems that their main aim was to enter the vast numbers of public houses and lodging houses in that vicinity in search of the Irish navvies. Having found several they beat them unmercifully.

The Englishmen were also accompanied by some women, some of them armed with vicious weapons, who were stimulating their men on to violence. When the mob reached the top of Westgate however they were met by the magistrates, and a large line strung across the road of specials backed by the Sheffield and Rotherham Yeomanry. The Riot Act was read out by Henry Walker, and they were ordered to disperse before they were charged by the special constables. It was reported that the Sheffield Yeomanry was commanded by Captain Jeffcock and the Rotherham Yeomanry by Lieutenant Swann.

The men and women refused to disperse and the militia was ordered to charge at them. It was later described that the Volunteers made a formidable line as they marched towards the rioters holding their weapons ready. The struggle was thankfully short and as a result the Englishmen broke ranks and scattered in all directions throughout the town. During the melee another of the magistrates who had assembled, Rev Mr Chandler saw an Irish man being attacked among the crowd. He gallantly rode forward on his horse and dragged the Irish man up onto his saddle and galloped off with him.

All the gentlemen who observed the resistance to the rioters were warm in their praise of the specials and the Yeomanry who had saved the town 'from all the excesses of lawless violence'. Just at the conclusion of the proceedings, Earl Fitzwilliam arrived from Sheffield where he had been consulting with the magistrates of that town on what emergency measures needed to be taken should the situation worsen. But with the rioters scattered and police combing the area for any of them that might have been left in the town, matters eventually quietened down. The Rotherham troop of Yeomanry remained in the town until the Friday making frequent patrols to prevent any problems arising. Thirty-one of the rioters were taken to the court house and placed in the cells.

On Thursday evening about 6 pm the prisoners were brought before the magistrates and Earl Fitzwilliam. The Earl spoke to each of them separately trying to convince them of their unreasonable behaviour. Some of them expressed contrition, and as a consequence twenty six of the prisoners were instantly dismissed. It was hoped that by showing such mercy that it would have a good effect on their compatriots. The remaining five prisoners, who were thought to be the ringleaders in the proceedings, were kept in custody. Their names were George Wilson, James Richardson, Charles Johnson, George Fisher and Thomas York.

When Earl Fitzwilliam was returning back to his estate at Wentworth, he met a group of angry English labourers. They had been sent to find out the fate of the five prisoners, who they believed had already been sent to Wakefield gaol for 12 month imprisonment. He assured them that they had not yet been dealt with, and told them if they returned to work and conducted themselves peaceably, the men would soon be liberated. The

Englishmen dispersed, but rumours reached the ears of Mr Bland that a second attempt would be made to rescue the five prisoners that night. For their own safety they too were dispatched to Sheffield under armed guard that same evening.

On Friday morning 12 October there were more reports that many more Englishmen were congregating in the neighbourhood of Swinton. They had been joined by a party of navvies from Wakefield who had walked down the line. It was also reported that another contingent from Eckington was shortly expected. Persons were sent out to watch their movements, and to report any indication of an advance towards Rotherham. However the party's were dispersed and gradually the men agreed to go back to work. It was decided that special constables would be stationed at intervals along the route to offer protection for the contractors and the labourers who were now back working on the railway.

Meanwhile many of the Irish who had spent the night at Sheffield were arriving back in the town. Most of them just collected their wages, before leaving the town for good and moved on to seek work elsewhere. Matters seemed to have settled somewhat as the shopkeepers opened up their shops and business of the town returned. Scouts came into the town at frequent intervals to report that all was quiet upon the line in all directions and it was eventually felt that the riot had been quelled. Mr Swanick the engineer for the North Midland, Sheffield and Rotherham Railways went to Wentworth to consult with Earl Fitzwilliam. They put plans together to ensure that all the men now working on the lines would be protected by the special constables. Another special force from the Metropolitan police was also sent from London, to 'put an end to the lawlessness of the proceedings'.

On Monday 15 October1838 the five men were brought back from Sheffield and placed before the magistrates at Rotherham. Mr Bland told the court that the riot had been peacefully extinguished. Irish workers had not resumed their work on the railways, and many of them had already left the town. Four of the men who had expressed contrition were release, apart from

George Wilson. He was seen as the ringleader in the riot and had been instrumental in releasing the prisoner at Swinton. Eight London policemen arrived in Rotherham on Sunday 21 October to undertake the direction of the force of special constables who would afford protection for the men now working on the railway line. It was believed that the measures taken 'will prevent any further riotous behaviour on the part of the navvies and quash them before they have a chance to start'.

George Wilson was sent to take his trial at the Sheffield Quarter Sessions, where he appeared on 20 October 1838. He was charged with riot and the assault on Mr Bland to which he pleaded guilty. Lord Wharncliffe cross examined him to ascertain what was the object of those involved in the riot. He told his Lordship that it was one of his companions who had been struck by the pick, which had started the riot. They were then told that the Irish were going to drive the English navvies from the railway line. Lord Wharncliffe told him:

'You have committed a breach of the peace, firstly by assembling in a riotous manner with other persons and secondly by rescuing a prisoner from the hands of the officers. It is therefore the duty of this court to pass sentence upon you, and to show the country that it is determined to do its duty in these respects, and that the public peace is not to be broken with impunity.

We are informed by one of the magistrates who was present, that although you appeared as a ringleader of the riotous party, you did not behave in a totally savage manner, as to call for severe punishment. We would fain hope from the circumstances of your pleading guilty that you are sensible of having committed a great offence against the laws of your country. Under the circumstances the court is willing to pass a lenient sentence'.

He was then sentenced to just six months imprisonment with hard labour and so ended the Rotherham Railway Riot. But fear of the repetition of such rioting did not go away so easily.

A memorial was signed by a large number of the most respectable inhabitants of the town of Rotherham, Rawmarsh, Wath and the areas adjacent to the North Midland Railway, asking for a detachment of soldiers to be permanently stationed in Rotherham. The petition was forwarded to the Secretary of State, but as peace was restored it was decided that they were not needed.

The line from Sheffield to Rotherham was successfully opened on Wednesday 31 October 1838 and Earl Fitzwilliam was present. It was reported that 'Mr Stephenson and a party of friends travelled to Rotherham from Sheffield by a Victory engine in just 9 minutes'. A few days later it was announced that a regular daily service had now been established and the trains will now run every hour between the two towns.

Chapter Two: Drunken brawl at the Bridge Inn.

In any research into local crime, a researcher will find that many of the crimes committed in the Victorian period had their basis in drunkenness. Throughout the Victorian era, Temperance Movements were prevalent in Britain, and Parliament was lobbied on many occasions to have public house opening hours decreased. Rotherham was no different in supporting a demand that they be closed altogether on Sundays. Although the Temperance Movement certainly found some support in Rotherham, they were usually unpopular with many of the working class men and woman. As a consequent crimes which were fuelled by alcohol continued.

Thankfully most of these were trivial and few ended in murder. One which did however, took place right outside the historic Bridge Inn. The inn is placed near to the Chapel on the Bridge which has been in existence for over six hundred years. During that time many visitors and pilgrims to Rotherham have passed over the bridge to enter into the town of Rotherham. Today the inn, which at one time was known as Nellie Deans, serves traditional ales in a friendly and cheerful atmosphere. Such is its popularity that it has won awards, and has been featured in Good Beer Guide. Back in 1839 the pub had its own brew house, and it was there that the body of a man was taken after being struck down on the very bridge, after which it was named.

On Tuesday evening 6 August 1839 about 6 pm, Isaac Lee was walking back into Rotherham from Masbrough after finishing work there. He was approaching the bridge over the river when he saw three people, two men and a woman standing there. Suddenly a third person approached and Lee was horrified to see one of the men, who he learned later was called Joseph Pike hitting the newcomer William Shackleton several times across the face. Another witness called John Doe, a blacksmith of Masbrough, also saw the men brawling, as he too was returning back into the town.

He noted that the newcomer was very drunk and he was staggering and cursing. He was so enraged that he was almost foaming at the mouth, but Doe could not tell what he was saying. Lee who was closer, saw the man Pike walk towards Shackleton and say to him 'thou's blackguarded me for a long time, and now I'll pay thee for it'. He saw Pike hit the drunken man on the face with his right hand, and then immediately again with his left hand. Doe went over to stop the attack as he could see that the victim was clearly drunk. He looked at the attacker and said to him 'for shame of yourself for using the man so'.

The victim was not about to give up however. He got to his feet and clapping his hands together saying 'thou hast paid a sovereign at Doncaster, and thou shall pay another one for this', referring to a fine which Pike had recently had to pay. Pike immediately started forward again and told Shackleton 'well I will not pay it for nowt then' and he struck the man very hard once again, this time he knocked him to the floor. Doe noted that he hit him on the right side of the face again near to his ear.

Both men watched in horror as Shackleton fell down onto his left side, in the middle of the bridge and this time he stayed down. They could both see that he was now bleeding from the nose and mouth, and that he was clearly badly injured. Isaac Lee said to Pike in disgust at that point 'I hope thou'll be satisfied now; thou hast finished him'. He saw at that point that all the anger had left Pike, who now looked anxious, as if he had just realised what he had done. John Doe dropped to his knees to inspect the man on the ground. He appeared to be completely insensible and Doe was not sure at that point whether Shackleton was alive or not.

Isaac Lee stated that he would find him a doctor and then he ran up Bridgegate and into the town centre. Pike also said that he would find a doctor and he ran to the house of surgeon Mr Wilkinson. The surgeon asked him what was the matter, and Pike told him that there was a man on the bridge who was bleeding badly. When Mr Wilkinson asked the cause, he told him that the man had used abusive language at him and that he had 'pushed him down'. The surgeon asked Pike if he was still lying on the bridge and hearing that he was, he directed his assistant James Woodhead to return with Pike and examine him. He told his assistant to see what was the matter, and to get the victim to a place of safety and off the ground. When the two men got back to the bridge Mr Woodhead went inside the Bridge Inn and asked the landlord, Mr Ridgeway to allow him to bring Shackleton inside. Mr Ridgeway told him that he could put the man in the brew house where there was some chairs.

When Mr Woodhead returned back to the surgery he told Mr Wilkinson what had happened, and the surgeon went to the brew house himself to see the patient about nine o'clock that same night. Mr Wilkinson found William Shackleton still insensible, and still lying uncomfortably on four wooden chairs. He berated the landlord for behaving so inhumanely towards an injured man, and he ordered that he be put into a bed in one of the rooms of the inn. When this had been accomplished, Mr Wilkinson examined him more carefully. He found that the patient was clearly labouring under concussion of the brain, as well as the effects of liquor and loss of blood.

The surgeon attended him at the Bridge Inn until Thursday morning about ten o'clock when he arrived and found his patient in a dying condition. William Shackleton died within minutes of Mr Wilkinson's arrival and Joseph Pike aged 31 was taken into custody charged with causing his death. An inquest was held at the Rotherham Court House on Friday 9 August 1839 at 9 am on the body of the deceased man by the local Coroner. The case was watched by a local solicitor Mr Joseph Badger for the prisoner, who was still in the cells in custody. After the jury had been sworn in, they went to the premises at the Bridge Inn where they viewed the body of William Shackleton.

The first witness was Isaac Lee who testified to the assault. He described how Joseph Pike had hit William Shackleton 'with all his might' on the ear or on the side of the neck. A juror asked him

17

if Shackleton had struck out at Pike at all, but the witness told him that he had not, in fact he made no resistance at all. Lee stated that he had not clearly heard any words pass between the deceased and Pike, before he saw the latter strike out at him. He said he never saw Shackleton strike at Pike at all as far as he could tell. Lee told the jury clearly that 'it was not an accidental blow or a push' and that Pike had lashed out at the deceased man quite deliberately.

He condemned the prisoner with his next sentence as he stated that 'he did it coolly and not as if in a great passion'. Lee was asked by a member of the jury to clarify if he thought that Pike was drunk at the time he assaulted the deceased man. The witness shook his head and stated that 'he seemed to me to be sober'. John Doe was the next to gave his evidence and he admitted that he too had not seen the start of the fight, and did not know the reason why the two men had been fighting. When he was cross examined by Mr Joseph Badger, he told him that there seemed to be no provocation and that Shackleton did not assume a fighting stance, or try to protect himself in any way.

Another witness was a man called James Hancock who stated that he was at the other side of the bridge coming away from Rotherham towards Masbrough, when he heard men shouting. He saw a man going over the bridge, heading for the road leading towards Rawmarsh. It was very clear that the man was in a very intoxicated state as he walked towards the bridge, and standing on it were some people. Hancock heard the man make some comment about 'a guinea' in an irritating manner, and he heard Pike say something which he did not understand in reply.

At the time Pike was leaning against the wall of the bridge, and was accompanied by two other persons. At first the two men were together in the middle of the bridge, but then Hancock saw Shackleton walk away before turning round again. At that point Pike left his companions and the two men walked towards each other, still in a very angry manner. The witness heard Pike say 'thou does not appear to be quiet, but I will quieten thee' before he struck him over the temple with his right hand and then again with his left. Then he gave him a blow which struck him so hard that it turned him completely around, and he fell violently onto his left side.

Hancock told the Coroner that the deceased was very drunk, but Pike seemed to be quite calm and not drunk at all. Hancock described how he had knelt down beside the injured man and took hold of his head. Seeing the serious condition he was in, with blood coming from his nose and mouth, Hancock said to Pike:

'I do believe that thou hast killed the man. I never saw a more vicious stroke in my life. You appear to be in a cool blood, and to hit a poor innocent, intoxicated man in that way was wrong and brutal. If the man does die I will come from Sheffield to attend the inquest to give evidence against you'.

Shortly after this the man was removed away from the centre of the bridge, Hancock still holding his head whilst Pike and Lee carried him to the brew house. Hancock told the inquest that after the assault, he also noted a great change in Pike as if he truly regretted his actions. He went to fetch a medical man and when the surgeon's assistant arrived and began to bleed Shackleton, Pike held the basin with shaking hands. He told the inquest 'I never saw a man more desirous for the relief of the deceased than Pike was'.

Another man appeared as a witness and gave his name as John Roberts of Ball Street, Green Lane, Sheffield. He told the Coroner that he had known Pike for six or seven years. He and his wife had travelled to Rotherham on that Tuesday evening, and as they were walking towards the town they saw Pike. Roberts described how they all stood talking on the bridge, when a man who he didn't know passed them, and said something to Pike about asking him for a job many times before. The man who was clearly drunk then started to use a great deal of abusive language. Roberts told him to hold his tongue in front of his wife, and Pike pushed away the man saying that he wanted nothing more to do with him.

19

Shackleton walked off, but after about twenty yards he returned and Pike swung at him. Roberts stated that the blow 'would not have killed a worm' but the drunken man almost immediately fell to the ground. Unlike the previous witnesses, he claimed that Shackleton was preparing to defend himself, and had walked back towards Pike in a fighting stance. Roberts described how the surgeon had examined the man, and eventually his wife and himself had left the scene and continued on with their business in Rotherham.

He told the court that the day after the assault and before Shackleton had died, that Pike had gone to his house at Sheffield. He explained that it was not thought that the man would live, and stated that 'it was a bad job and he wished it had never happened'. Pike had asked Roberts to appear for him if the man should die and there was an inquest, to which Roberts had agreed that he would. The two men discussed the events of what had happened the previous night. Pike told Roberts to 'speak the truth at the inquest' and to carefully describe what he had seen.

The witnesses wife, Charlotte Roberts then gave her evidence and confirmed much of her husband's testimony. She told the inquest 'I curbed Pike for striking out at a drunken man, and if I could have prevented it, I should'. She claimed the blow was only 'a side blow', but nevertheless it was strong enough to knock down the inebriated man. Mr Wilkinson told the Coroner that he had examined the deceased whilst he was still alive, and had found a slight external injury on the left side of his head, a little behind the ear.

The surgeon said that the left side of the man's face was swollen and the left eye was black as if he had taken a severe beating. He stated that very morning he had made a post mortem examination, and found extraversion of blood on the whole of the right side of the brain. There was no fracture of the skull and the whole of the deceased man's viscera was healthy. In answer to a question from one of the jury, the surgeon answered that 'being intoxicated, the fall was sufficient to cause his death, without any propelling force being added'.

The solicitor watching the case for Joseph Pike, was Mr Badger and he asked Mr Wilkinson if the fact that the man was drunk would have cause greater extraversion in the brain, than would have been the case with a sober man, to which Dr Wilkinson agreed. At that point Joseph Pike was brought into the court room, accompanied by two constables, and the depositions which had been given by the witnesses were read out to him.

The Coroner told the prisoner that he need not make a statement unless he wanted to, and cautioned Pike that anything he said, might be taken down and used in evidence against him. The prisoner however seemed determined to put his side of the story as he told the inquest:

'I was standing on the bridge talking to a man called Joseph Roberts and his wife when Shackleton came up and started being abusive to me [...] I pushed him away and said I did not want any of his bother. He then went about thirty yards away from me before coming back again, clapping his hands and raising his fists. I then gave him a shove, and he tumbled down by the shove that I gave him'.

By now the enquiry had lasted till one o'clock, and it was therefore adjourned to later that same evening when the jury met again to hear the evidence read over, and to consider their judgment. After consulting a short time the jury returned a verdict of manslaughter against Joseph Pike. The Coroner issued a warrant for the committal of the prisoner to York, in order to take his trial at the next assizes. On August 17 Pike along with seven others was removed to the Castle at York to await his trial.

He was brought before judge Mr Justice Erskine on Tuesday 17 March 1840 where he pleaded guilty. After all the evidence had been heard, it would seem that the assize jury were more lenient towards the prisoner than the Coroner's inquest had been. They

21

found him guilty, but asked for mercy because of the strong provocation to which the prisoner had been subjected to. His Lordship in summing up pointed out that because the victim had been drunk at the time, he might have fallen more heavily than a sober man might have done.

Warning Joseph Pike against his future behaviour, he pointed out that 'you might have come before me on a much more serious charge than that you face today'. The judge told him that as he had already been a prisoner for seven months, he ordered that he was to be imprisoned for just a further ten days. It was reported that Joseph Pike looked very relieved.

Joseph Pike would have been very thankful to have left the dock with the judge's warning ringing in his ears. He could so easily have been charged with murder, which as a capital offence might have probably resulted in the death penalty. It does seem from the reports that Pike showed a genuine remorse for his actions, and by his swift summons to the surgeons assistant, he managed to get medical aid for the injured man as quickly as possible. Other prisoners in the same position who showed little remorse for their actions were dealt much more severely by the courts.

Chapter Three: Stealing Rabbits from Masbrough Station.

As we have already seen by May of 1840 the North Midland Railway had extended as far as Rotherham, and on the 11 May the opening ceremony at Masbrough Station had been performed. The weather was rainy to the point where the local newspaper said that 'even the wetness of the weather did not dampen the excitement of the day'. Now local people could travel to Sheffield in 15 minutes. However as the trade became busier, the opportunities for theft increased. One such crime was committed in Rotherham on Sunday night of 15 November 1840.

A parcel porter for the North Midland Railway, George Cuttmore spotted a hamper of tame rabbits waiting on the platform at Masbrough for the next train to Sheffield. The hamper had been taken off the last train from York and the label stated that it was sent by a Miss Charlotte Pinder to be delivered to a Mr John Smith. Any parcels or livestock that was transported on these trains were seen to be the property of the Railway Company and were properly dealt with when any theft or infringement occurred. However some saw it, not as theft but more as an advantage of the job.

Seeing the hamper, Cuttmore went over to a switch man called John Bagshaw and asked him if he could take a rabbit or two as he pointed at the hamper. Bagshaw told the porter that he couldn't and as Cuttmore moved away he appeared very disgruntled, saying that 'one or two would not be missed'. Bagshaw knew that Cuttmore was in the habit of making jokes, so he did not take him too seriously at first. However later the switch man saw the porter opening the hamper, but when Cuttmore saw that he was being observed, he closed the lid quickly and walked away.

Bagshaw spotted him later moving the hamper to another darker part of the platform and then he saw the man put something into his pocket, but he could not be sure that it had been taken out of the hamper. The porter was next seen putting the hamper into the guards van on the Sheffield train. When his shift at the Masbrough station ended, Bagshaw was sure that the porter had something under his coat. He was very suspicious and although he did not wish to report Cuttmore officially, he mentioned the matter to the night watchman James Castle, before he too went off duty.

John Chambers the guard on the train from Masbrough to Sheffield remembered Cuttmore putting the hamper onto the train when it stopped at Masbrough Station. Although the guard saw it in the van, he did not know what it contained at the time, although he was told later it was some rabbits. He noted as he stacked it in the van that the hamper was wrapped in brown paper and had been tied up with string. The label which was stuck on the top of the hamper appeared to be torn, as if it had been opened. When the train arrived at Sheffield, the hamper was locked in the parcels office for the night.

Meanwhile Elizabeth Downing who was employed at the Black Bull in Masbrough saw Cuttmore coming into the pub on the Sunday night when he finished work. When she served him his ale, he jokingly asked her to put her hand in his pocket, and she screamed when she felt something warm that had grey fur. Cuttmore laughed at her and she laughed with him, as he was well known for his joking. He later maintained that it was a hairy cap that he had in his pocket, although he never showed it to her.

The next morning, the owner of the hamper Mr Smith had gone to the station at Sheffield, and had complained that some of the rabbits were missing. On Tuesday when Bagshaw was told about the theft, he spoke with the watchman James Castle, and as a result of that conversation they both confronted Cuttmore. The porter claimed that he had not stolen anything out of the hamper and angrily he claimed that both of them were trying to ruin him by making allegations about his honesty.

John Chambers the guard of the Sheffield train also spoke to Cuttmore stating that he had seen him put the hamper onto the Sheffield train and asked him if he had taken any rabbits out of it. Cuttmore at first denied it and then after he had time to think about it, offered to pay for the stolen rabbits. When Chambers declined, Cuttmore then offered to resign from his post, but the guard told him that he would have to report the conversation about the theft. Matters moved swiftly at that point.

John Sharman the Inspector of the Railway Police went to the porter and charging him with the crime, took Cuttmore into custody. When he was taking him to the police station at Rotherham, Cuttmore urged the Inspector to let him escape. He promised him that 'if he could get at liberty he would cut from there and go out of the country'. Inspector Sharman told him that he could not do that and he handed his prisoner over to the police authorities in Rotherham and the man was placed in a cell.

George Cuttmore was brought before the magistrates on Monday 23 November 1840 charged with the theft from the North Midland Railway. Mr Vickers appeared on behalf of the Railway Company, and Mr Joseph Badger appeared for the defence. His defence solicitor cross examined the switch man John Bagshaw and asked him if the train stopped anywhere else on its way from York and was told that it stopped at Wakefield. Mr Badger suggested to him that the theft could have quite possibly have taken place at Wakefield as at Masbrough.

John Sawyer of Sheffield stated that he was in the parcels office at Sheffield station and was in the habit of receiving consignments of rabbits and other livestock on a regular basis. He stated that when the hamper was delivered, he too noticed that the brown paper had been torn. After listening to all the evidence, George Cuttmore was found guilty and Mr Badger asked the court for bail. It was granted, but as the prisoner was unable to produce sureties of £25, he remained in custody.

George Cuttmore was among other prisoners from Rotherham who were taken to Wakefield Gaol on Thursday 26 November to await their trial. The porter appeared at the West Riding Sessions held at Doncaster on Tuesday 11 January 1841 in front of the magistrate Mr W B Wrightson. He was charged with stealing the rabbits, the property of the Railway Company. The prosecution was Sir G Lewin and he pointed out that

'although the property in this case was of small value, it could never be a trifling thing for a servant to rob its master. If the Railway Companies did not occasionally make examples in these cases, there would be no security for any of the property committed to their charge'.

When the switch man John Bagshaw was cross examined by the defence Mr Baines, he asked him why he had not reported the theft at the time. The witness said that the prisoner was a man known for joking and he wasn't sure if he was simply winding him up. Only when the theft came to light did he tell his superiors. Charlotte Pinder of York proved that when she sent the hamper it had contained 21 rabbits. The recipient, Mr Smith stated that when he opened the hamper at the Bradley coach office in Sheffield, it only contained 17 rabbits.

When the magistrates asked Cuttmore what he had to say to the charge, he stated that he was not guilty, but added that it would ruin his character to have the charge proved against him. Mr Baines addressed the jury and told them that there was no absolute proof that the prisoner had indeed stolen the rabbits, as no one had actually seen him do it. There was no account of what had happened to the parcel when it arrived at Wakefield, nor after it had been delivered to the parcel clerk in Sheffield. He denounced Bagshaw's evidence as 'unworthy of credit'. However the magistrate saw this differently and sentenced George Cuttmore to six weeks imprisonment.

Chapter Four: The Toll Bar Robberies.

In the eighteenth and nineteenth century Britain the roads of the country were in such a poor condition that turnpike trusts were set up to repair and maintain the roads of each county. A group of respectable people were set up as trustees by individual Acts of Parliament and they were responsible for each section of the road. These trustees were of their very nature selected from the groups of gentlemen and clergy, and they in turn employed clerks, solicitors and surveyors. In order to pay for the improvements, the trustees had the power for the collection of tolls from each person using the road.

These collection points had toll booths erected and a board which showed the list of tolls were displayed at each one. There was a set price to pay for coaches, carts and droves of animals going through the turnpikes and, although there was a great improvement in the road system of the country, they became very unpopular. Most people resented the fact that they now had to pay for what had been free before. The toll houses also varied from one county to another. Some, which still exist today, can be seen as small cottages where the toll collector lived with his wife.

Naturally there were some of the criminal fraternity who saw these toll booths, and the money they contained, to be easy prey and they were regularly robbed with great savagery. In Rotherham there existed a notorious gang which had preyed on these toll bars for a very long time. However to the relief of the police authorities this gang was finally captured. A little after one o'clock on the morning of the 7 February 1843, a toll keeper, Pickles Roberts and his wife were in bed at the Broomhill toll bar near Rotherham. He heard the sounds of horses hooves coming from the direction of the town, before hearing a shout of 'gate' which was the cry for him to open the toll bar.

Getting out of bed he put on his slippers and great coat and went to open the gate. He saw the man on a horse standing by the bar and recognised him as George Storey. He was putting the key to the lock to open the gate, when he saw four other men coming around the corner of the toll bar house. Realising he was about to be robbed, he ran back to his own door, but one of the men, who he recognised as a man called William Hall, hit him over the head, crying out 'go at him lads' and he beat Roberts savagely. Eventually some of the men went into the house leaving him in the custody of Hall and Storey.

Still struggling outside, Roberts managed to break free as he knew he had to save his wife who was still in bed. He dashed into the house where he saw a man he knew as Robert Ridge searching through a chest of drawers with a lantern in his hand. He saw another man going into the ground floor room called the parlour, where his wife was and he knew she would be afraid. Roberts attempted to stop him, but was savagely attacked once again. This time he was held by three men, Hall and Storey and another man, whilst the others searched the premises.

His wife Mary saw through a little window in the wall, a man come through the house door and approach the door to the parlour. He was accompanied by other men and she noted that one of them had a large cudgel in his hand. She heard her husband shout out 'murder' and she ran to the door to try to bar the man's entrance, but he already had his head and shoulders through the door. Mary saw her husband put his arms around the man and pull him away from the door to the parlour. She then looked through the little window and saw the three men in the house, looking through the little window back at her and became very afraid.

She identified one of the men as William Pressley and another, who was holding the lantern, as Robert Ridge, who she saw with horror had a hatchet on his shoulders. She begged them 'Mester, please don't hurt him' nodding towards her husband. Robert Ridge told her 'we wont hurt him if you come out and tell us where the money is'. She went out into the room where the men were, and went to the drawer where the money was kept. Ridge already had one hand in the drawer and held the lantern with his other hand.

28

She asked him if he had already found it, and he told her 'no' as he thrust the lantern at her. She took it and held it up to his face and as soon as he noticed what she was doing, he took the lantern away from her and pushed her aside.

She took out the money and gave it to the men, however they said that 'it was not enough and they would have some more'. Mary told him that it was all they had in the house, and eventually they took away the money which amounted to £3.5s.7d in copper and silver. The men then left, but their nights robbery was not finished yet. They proceeded to another toll bar at Aldwarke where they again shouted for the gate man John Rannard. His wife Elizabeth later made a statement where she described the attack. She said that:

'between 2 and 3 o'clock on the morning of the 8 February, I heard a person call out 'gate'. My husband immediately got up and put on his coat and slippers and went out. I heard him cry out 'murder'. I ran to his assistance and saw him outside the house and three men striking him with something like a bludgeon, and two other men holding him. Then my husband was lying on the ground, and there was a mass of blood about him. They pushed me into my bedroom, which was on the ground floor. One of them had a lantern in his hand, and he proceeded to ransack the drawers and turning to me, he twice said. "your money you bugger, or I'll blow your brains out".

I said "the money is not there, but spare my husband". There was a light shining on the drawer, so I could see very well. We then came out of the bedroom into the house and I said "my money is there" pointing to the desk and I cried "but let me go to my husband". The prisoner Ridge said "damn you, your husband is safe". The prisoners Hancock and Storey were two of the men engaged. I saw Hall take the money out of a little drawer in the desk, and out of a little basket and offer part of it to the prisoner Pressley. They took away nearly £5. I then went out and found my husband lying on the ground and his head was a mass of blood'.

29

Henry Womack who was the keeper of the lock-up was on duty at the Police Station at Rotherham that night. About four o'clock in the morning of the 8 February, he had received some information which sent him straight to the Aldwarke toll bar. In his statement which he made soon afterwards he described the scene:

'I went into the bedroom of the bar-house and there saw John Rannard the bar-keeper in bed, bleeding from his head. He appeared very much ill-used. I saw in the same room a woman's night gown, and a man's topcoat, very bloody. I also observed blood on the floor, and traced it to the flags outside the house, where I found upon a hollow flag, a pool of blood. I also found a larger stick marked with blood. Rannard and his wife said they had been robbed and ill-used by six or seven men wearing fustian jackets. Mrs Rannard said that she should know some of the men again, that she scuffled with in the house. I traced some footprints from the bar towards Aldwarke'.

Police Sergeant Daniel Astwood of Sheffield also made a later statement saying that having heard the identification of the men from the witnesses on the following night after the robbery:

'in consequence of some information which had been received, myself and Police Sergeant Blackburn and two watchmen went to the house of the man Pressley in a yard near to Willey Street, Sheffield. He was in bed. I called him up and told him to dress himself. I searched the house and on the bed in the chamber I found a fustian jacket. I brought Pressley to the Sheffield Town Hall'.

Pressley was removed to Rotherham and brought before the magistrates on Monday 13 February 1843 where the Chief Constable of Rotherham, Mr John Bland described how he had received William Pressley into custody earlier that morning. Mary Roberts gave her evidence, but was unable to recognise the prisoner who was now wearing a smock frock. She had described the fustian jackets that the men had been wearing, and said that the one she thought the prisoner had been wearing had a turned up collar. Constable Daniel Astwood had brought the fustian jacket into the court room, which he had found at Pressley's house earlier that morning and requested that the prisoner put it on.

Bland turned the collar up but Pressley under the pretence of adjusting it, turned the collar down again. Mr Hoyle asked that the there was insufficient evidence against the prisoner and asked that he be remanded, but the bench told him that they would like him to be seen by another witness. Mrs Rannard also was called and she immediately recognised him as the man she had seen at 2.30 am on Wednesday morning at her house. She was extremely agitated as she made this identification stating that he was one of the men who had left her husband for dead.

In order for the police to establish who Pressley's comrades were and to elicit more information on the case, an advertisement was inserted in the local newspapers which read:

£150 Reward

ROBBERY AT ALDWARKE & BROOMHILL TOLL BARS
Whereas on TUESDAY NIGHT the 7 February 1843, about One o'clock, Five Men entered the TOLL house at ALDWARKE BAR, near Rotherham, and Stole therefrom a Sum of MONEY, and cruelly used the Collector and his Wife. On the same night the BROOMHILL TOLL HOUSE was also Entered by the same number of Persons, who ill used the Collector and Plundered the House, taking away all the Money therein. Four of the Men wore caps and Fustian Jackets and one of them was remarkably tall.

A REWARD of £100 will be paid by her Majesty's Secretary of State, in addition from the Sum of £25 from Mr JOSHUA BOWER the younger, and the sum of £25 from the Trustees of the Tinsley and Doncaster Turnpike Road, to any Person or Persons who shall give such information and evidence as shall lead to the Conviction of the several parties. And the Secretary of State for the Home Department has authorised the offer of Her Majesty's most gracious PARDON to any accomplices (not being the

31

Person who actually ill used the Toll Collectors) who shall give such information as shall lead to the same result.

Information to be given to Mr John Bland, High Constable, Rotherham or to Mr W F HOYLE, Solicitor, Rotherham, Clerk to the Trustees of the said Tinsley and Doncaster Turnpike Road.

John Bland as a result of information received on the morning of the 16 February about 5 am, went with Henry Womack and Daniel Astwood to the house of Robert Ridge who lived near the cricket ground in Sheffield Park. There he found Ridge in bed and he told him to get up and get dressed warning him 'you are out this time, old chap'. Womack and Astwood searched the house and outbuildings whilst the prisoner was dressing. Ridge said to him 'I know what you have come about. You are about the bar robberies'. Bland said to him that he appeared to know something about them and arrested him. The prisoner was searched and a pick lock and keys were found on him.

Mr Bland was called to one of the outbuildings where Womack showed him where two life preservers were hidden. These were weapons described as being half a yard in length having a round ball of lead at the end making them a fearsome, heavy weapon. Ridge was brought back to Rotherham and was taken in front of the magistrates where the tools of his trade found on him at the time of his arrest and the life preservers were displayed to the court and the jury. These were laid out on the bench in front of the prisoner.

An hour later John Bland went back to Sheffield with information about the other suspects. He went out again with Womack and Astwood to a house in Hawley Croft, Sheffield and there he found William Hall, John Hancock and George Storey all still in bed. The men were arrested and they were brought back to Rotherham. Bland went to see William Pressley and asked him if he had any objection to him taking down in writing the statement he had made earlier that morning and Pressley agreed, saying that he wanted to tell the truth. The statement read:

Rotherham Lock Up.
16 February 1843

Last night I had an advertisement shown to me, promising a pardon to any accomplice concerned in the robbery of the Aldwarke and Broomhill toll bars. For the sake of my family I thought it best to speak the truth, in the hope of being allowed a pardon for so doing. On the night of the 7 February about 9 pm, I went to Robert Ridge's house in the Park at Sheffield and there I found Ridge, Charles Fullalove, George Storey, John Hancock and William Hall.

We sat talking until abut 10.30 pm when we all left Ridge's house and went along Cricket Inn Lane, then by the canal side to Attercliffe Bridge, then along the turnpike road till we got to Bentley's brewery. Ridge then led us across some fields to Moorgate and went into a stable and brought out a horse, which he led across some fields to Broom toll bar. When we go to the bar, Ridge helped Storey on the horse and he went up to the bar calling out 'gate'. The bar man came out and went to the gate when Hancock and Fullalove struck him and he cried out 'murder'.

Ridge went into the house, having an axe over his shoulders and I followed him, leaving Hancock and Fullalove fighting with the bar-man. Ridge asked where the money was. The bar-woman said it was in the drawer, and that she would get it if they did not hurt her husband. Ridge went to the drawer and took out the money. We then came out and the bar-man went in and shut the door and Ridge bid him "good night". The horse we left at the bar. Ridge then led us across some fields, saying we were going to another bar and we came out on the Doncaster Road, near to Eastwood. We all went onto the turnpike to Aldwarke bar.

We then went to a stable and Ridge unlocked the door and brought out a foal. He led it up to the door and called out 'gate'. The barman came out and Ridge immediately struck him with a

33

stick and he cried out "murder". I said "don't hit him. There are plenty of you to hold him". Ridge went into the house and I followed him. Ridge met the bar-woman in the passage and asked her where the money was. She said it was in the drawer in the house. Ridge had a lantern and he threw a light upon the drawer.

Hall took the money out of two little boxes, which were inside the drawer. He put one lot in my hand and the other he took himself. The bar-woman begged that we would not kill her husband. We all left and went across some fields to a shed near Aldwarke and then we shared the money. We had 22s each and 6d left over. We then took the canal side to Mexborough and Ridge threw the axe he had with him into the canal and then we went to Ridge's house. It was then about 6 am and we immediately separated and went home'.

As it was necessary for the men to have a horse with them when undertaking the robbery and to allay suspicion the men had decided to steal the animals they needed. It was later established that the horse that had been taken first had belonged to Mr Oxley and had been taken out of his stable on Moorgate.

The gang was brought into court on Monday 20 February 1843 before magistrates Colonel Fullerton, H Walker Esq., and Rev G Chandler, charged with breaking into the toll bar and ill using the toll bar keepers. The only one missing was Charles Fullalove who had absconded when the other men had been arrested and a warrant had been issued for his arrest. Pickles Roberts gave his evidence, and he described the men as all dressed in velveteen or fustian jackets, with caps on their heads which had been tied under their chins.

He was followed by the Chief Constable John Bland, who described how he had arrested the men in Sheffield and he read out the statement made by William Pressley. Pressley was then asked if he had anything more to add, he said:

'I have heard he statement read over which I made to Mr Bland concerning the robberies at Aldwarke and Broom toll bars. The statement is true. I made a confession in consequence of an advertisement which was shown to me'.

Robert Chester, the clerk to Mr Oxley of Rotherham told the court that he had been told on 18 February that a prisoner in the lock-up wished to make a confession and he went there and saw George Storey and William Pressley. The prisoners were brought into the room and Chester told Storey that he understood that he wished to make a confession. When Storey stated that he did, Chester was told that 'what ever he said to him would be used as evidence against him' and he too made a statement which read:

*'Rotherham Gaol
18 February 1843*

This is true information of George Storey after being cautioned that what he said would be used in evidence against him, in the presence of Womack the constable and William Pressley another prisoner. Nothing has been said to me to cause me to make this confession, but that I found the evidence brought against me by the Broom bar-man was true. We rode up to the Broom bar on a horse on the morning of the 7 or 8 February and called out 'gate'. There were Robert Ridge, William Hall, John Hancock, William Pressley and Charles Fullalove.

We went to a house three quarters of a mile from Rotherham. Ridge and Hall fetched the horse out of the stable. We then went across some fields to the turnpike road. Ridge asked me to get on the horse and ride up to the gate. I got on the horse and he called out 'gate'. The bar-man came out and was struck by someone. I think it was Hall and he was on the other side of the gate. I used no violence. The bar-man screamed out "murder" and knocked one of the party down. I believe Hancock knocked him down. Ridge, Hall, Pressley and Fullalove came out of the bar-house. I never went in, but stood at the door.

35

When they came out, one of them, I think it was Fullalove, said "Lets go towards Doncaster". We went along the lane to an old hovel and shared the money. We all went to Ridge's house in Sheffield Park and then went home. It was about six o'clock on Wednesday morning'.

After this statement was read out by the clerk, the magistrates asked all the prisoners if they had anything to say. The defence solicitor Mr Badger on the part of Ridge, Hall and Hancock replied that they had nothing to say. Story and Pressley said that they had made the statement in consequence of being shown the advertisement which offered Her Majesty's pardon to any accomplices who confessed. The same prisoners were then charged with the robbery at the Aldwarke Bar.

Mrs Elizabeth Rannard's statement was read to the court, and then her husband was called. He was described as an elderly man, who looked so ill that he was accommodated with a seat. His head was still bound up with bandages and he kept his hat on whilst giving his evidence. He was described as having the appearance of a man who had been severely abused. On being sworn he told the court that at one point one of the men had picked up a watch which had been in a case in the drawer, but his companions told him to put it down saying 'we want no watches, its money we want'.

He said that the men found upwards of £4 in silver, which they made off with. His evidence was the same as his wife's and only varied slightly in small details. When he stated that he had seen two men running past the window, he was asked if he saw those men in court and he immediately pointed out Hancock and Storey. At this point he became considerably agitated and said that 'he had those two men in my eyes ever since'. He described being attacked and being knelt upon by some of the men.

The five prisoners were found guilty and sent to take their trial at the York Assizes. The clerk told the magistrates that several persons from different parts of the neighbourhood who had recently been broken into, were waiting in the next room. Mr

Hoyle applied to the bench to allow them to be called into the court room so that they might have an opportunity of seeing whether they knew any of the prisoners. The prisoners were then mixed among other men in the room, and several individuals were called in, but none of them identified the prisoners.

William Pressley, Robert Ridge, John Hancock, George Storey and William Hall appeared at the York Assizes on Thursday 16 March 1843 in front of Justice Coltman and the first to give evidence was Pickles Roberts. He described the viciousness of the attack on him and his wife, and said that 'there were many marks remaining on the walls and doors of the toll house', illustrating the heavy blows which had missed him.

William Pressley, who had given evidence against his companions, admitted his part in the robbery and stated that he had agreed with Womack that the £150 reward money would be split between himself and the other constables. The jury found all the prisoners guilty and Ridge, as the ringleader was sentenced to 20 years. Hall, Hancock and Storey were sentenced to 15 years each. Pressley was discharged.

Four months later, Charles Fullalove aged 36 was brought into the magistrates court at Rotherham on Tuesday 11 July 1843 after he had finally been captured the previous Sunday at a relatives house at Thorpe. He had been found in a bed secreted under the bedclothes and he was arrested and taken immediately to Rotherham gaol.

Magistrate Mr H Walker produced a document certifying that a true bill had been found against him by the Grand Jury at the previous assizes, and he was duly committed to take his own trial at York. He appeared at the Yorkshire Assizes on Thursday 20 July 1843, in front of Mr Justice Cresswell where he was sentenced to 15 years transportation for his part in the Rotherham toll bar robberies.

So ended the exploits of this particular toll bar gang and due to the increase of the railways turnpike trusts and toll bars collecting money from travellers ceased altogether by by 1870s. They had always been unpopular and gradually the taking over of road repairs was made by local Highway Boards. Often to show their indignation, there were great celebrations by the local people as the toll gates were finally thrown open.

Chapter Five: Elizabeth Neale.

Giving birth in Victorian Britain was a dangerous business. Like mental health issues there was little understanding of germs or the need for hygiene during the birth process. If there was a lack of understanding about basic amenities, absolutely nothing was known about the state of a woman's mind, during and after pregnancy. When a woman had a history of familial, mental instability the outcome was not hopeful. Puerperal fever turned gentle women, who some believed their sole purpose in life was to give birth, into a very dangerous person indeed.

The relationship between mental disorder and motherhood is a far from recent development. A case was heard before the Coroner in August 1845 at the Rotherham workhouse, when a child appeared to have come to his death through it's own mother's ill treatment. Elizabeth Neale was a widow who lived on Wellgate, Rotherham and on 15 July she had given birth to a daughter, although the child was illegitimate. The father of the child was said to be a nephew, a boy aged only 16 years of age. Her mother-in-law, Sarah Neale had acted as midwife to the baby, which was a full grown, healthy female child.

On 27 July Sarah visited Elizabeth, who was surprised to be told that the child had died. Sarah looked at the child and saw that its lips were black, and suspected that Elizabeth had given the child something, but the new mother denied this saying she had only given it water. Two days later Elizabeth went to the sexton of the Parish Church and asked him to bury the child who she claimed had been still-born. The sexton, Thomas Broadhead told Elizabeth that he could not bury the child without a death certificate from a medical man, and at this information she appeared very distressed and ran away. The child was taken away and the Coroner informed of its death.

Soon after this Elizabeth began to act very wildly, hiding under the stairs of a neighbours house and threatening to kill herself.

Later she was only prevented from throwing herself in the River Don by two men. Police Officer William Hudson was approached by one of the men, who was a lock keeper, who told him that he had prevented a woman from drowning herself, but from something she had said, thought that she had thrown her baby in the river. The two men took a walk around the town and they spotted Elizabeth in High Street, Rotherham and the lock keeper pointed her out as the women who had tried to kill herself.

Hudson approached her, but before he could speak she clutched hold of his arm and said 'Oh dear, save me; I have done wrong to my child'. The woman appeared very frightened as he took her into custody and on the way to the gaol she begged him to have mercy on her. Elizabeth was put in the cells and because she had tried to take her life, Hudson sat with her as she was far too distressed to sleep, claiming that 'something' was running round the room. Around 4 am he was pouring some tea out of a teapot and Elizabeth became very distressed. When asked what had upset her, she told Hudson that she had given the child some water from her teapot

An inquest was held on the unnamed child by Mr. T. Badger Esq., on 30 July 1845 following a request that a post mortem be held on the body. This was carried out by a workhouse medical officer, Mr. Joseph H. Turner and three other medical men. The surgeon informed the jury that the child appeared very emaciated and they found the upper part of the throat and the oesophagus congested with blood, and suspected that the child had been given sulphuric acid. Elizabeth was assisted into the room and she too appeared very emaciated and did not seem to understand what was said to her.

The Coroner explained to her that it was Mr. Turner's opinion that the child had been given some corrosive matter to drink, and asked her if she had any statement to voluntarily make. At this Elizabeth seemed very distressed and cried out:

'Oh spare me Master, I am not altogether right in the head. It is a good way from right, and I am not always knowing what I do. I hope you will spare me. I have not knowledge at times to know what I am properly doing. I did it, not thinking I was doing any harm'.

The inquest was then adjourned for two days until scientific tests could be carried out by a chemist to clarify whether sulphuric acid had been used to kill the child.

When the inquest was reconvened in the evening of 1 August 1845, professional chemist Mr. J. Heywood of Sheffield gave evidence, who stated that he had examined the contents of the stomach of the child, but had found no evidence of sulphuric or any other acid. Indeed the only conclusion the jury could come to was that the prisoner had given the child a drink from the teapot which had been warming on the fire. By mistake, she might have given it to the child not realising that it was scalding hot. The Coroner stated that no reliance could be put on any of the prisoner's statements from the state of mind she was in at the time.

The jury were told the illness she was suffering from might be hereditary and that she had a brother who was confined in a lunatic asylum at Derby and both her father and grandmother had died insane. On the suggestion from the Coroner, the jury returned an open verdict 'that the child had died from inflammation of the stomach, but how produced there was no satisfactory evidence to show'. The jury also expressed an opinion that the prisoner was not in a fit state of mind to be at large in the town, and the Coroner assured them that he would see that she was properly taken care of.

It is likely that Elizabeth Neale was probably taken to the lunatic ward of the Rotherham workhouse and confined there for her own safety. There is little doubt that she had killed her child, but probably without any intention to do so. Faced with the consequences of her crime and having no idea what to do with the

41

little body, she had tried to have it legally buried at the Parish Church, using the lie that it had been still-born as a reason. What desperate thoughts went through her mind after her baby died, for the two days before she approached the church sexton can only be imagined.

Chapter Six: Lady Barton.

One of the most formidable criminals I have come across during my research was that of a woman named Maria Barton who was known, for some unknown reason, as Lady Barton. She was a disreputable character who kept lodging houses and brothels and she also became a fence for stolen property, encouraging young local boys to steal. She was without doubt a bane on the Rotherham police force for many years.

Throughout the nineteenth century many people were called into court accused of keeping 'a house of ill-fame', or 'a disorderly house' which were Victorian euphemism's for brothels. These houses also held lodgers and were usually situated in the more disreputable part of the town. The newspapers reported that the keepers of such houses would often entice young girls into a life of debauchery. These girls were kept in such houses, and the brothel keepers would clothe and feed them, all of which had to be paid for. Brothels in Rotherham were usually the scene of many robberies, as the clientele were often drunk when they arrived. These activities would ensure that they would be closely watched by the constables on duty in the town.

The attention of the police was called to these dwellings, usually by so called 'respectable ratepayers'. In the first quarter of the century these were quickly dealt with when magistrates would drop all charges, if the accused prisoner agreed to leave the area. Maria Barton kept such a 'house' in a yard at Millgate, Rotherham, and was first mentioned in local newspapers in January 1839. She was charged with being the keeper of 'a house of ill fame' and she was arrested and was brought into custody. The charges were dropped when she promised to leave the area.

Seemingly she did so for a short time, but when the affair had blown over, Maria Barton returned back to Rotherham and resumed her former profession. She was still working at this professions by January 1845, when she was again brought into the magistrates court charged with the same crime. Maria was required to find sureties for herself of £20 and two others of £10 each to appear at the next Intermediate Sessions at Sheffield. She was brought into court on Saturday 1 March 1845, but this time she was defended by local solicitor, Mr Overend.

Superintendent John Bland gave evidence that he had known Maria Barton for ten years and during that time, with the exception of a few years when she left the town, she had

'kept a house of the most disorderly and dissolute character. I could state this from the class of persons whom I have seen there, many of whom were persons of the most abandoned character. Others were person of the most suspicious character, several of whom I knew had been convicted of felonies and other offences'.

He stated that the present prosecution was brought by the parish authorities, at the instance of the Rotherham magistrates. He continued to say that the prisoner and her house had represented the 'most perfect nuisance to the most respectable inhabitants of Rotherham'. After hearing evidence from some of these persons, the jury found Maria Barton guilty, and she was sentenced to be imprisoned and kept to hard labour for twelve months. By this point Maria Barton had already become a thorn in the side of the Rotherham police authorities that she was even mentioned in the Police Meeting the following month.

The ratepayers gathered to receive the report of Superintendent, Mr Bland. His elation over the imprisonment of his nemesis was palpable, when he tells the ratepayers that reports showed that year that incidents of general crime had been reduced in the town. He stated that he hoped that a further reduction in numbers would take place in the next year, as the 'greatest receptacle' in the town for such purposes had been broken up 'and the keeper Maria Barton had been prosecuted and convicted'. His elation was short lived.

Three years later Maria Barton was still causing problems for the legal authorities. On Monday 21 August 1848 She was brought before the court in Rotherham again this time charged with selling ale without a licence at the brothel on Millgate. In attendance was a representative from the Board of Excise, called Mr Broomhead. Evidence had been given by a man named Robert Winter who stated himself to be a miner from Dodworth, but was later found to have been 'leading a vagabond life' for the previous six months.

He claimed that on Sunday 1 July he came to Rotherham to give evidence against another prisoner at the Sessions and had slept at Mrs Barton's house that night. After attending the court, Winter went back to the house on Millgate and asked Mrs Barton if she could get him a pint of ale. She told him that she could and brought him a pint downstairs for which he paid her 2d. He had asked for another and she had gone upstairs to fetch for him, when Police Constable Hudson came into the house looking for two prostitutes. Winter called up the stairs for Barton telling her that 'the police were in the house' and she returned without the ale.

He was cross examined by Mr Broomhead who asked him when he had given in the statement against Mrs Barton. Winter replied that after the visit of the police to the house in Millgate, he and the two wanted prostitutes had left the house surreptitiously and he paid a visit for two or three days to the Ecclesfield Feast in Sheffield. Only then did he decide to go to the Excise office and laid the information against Maria Barton. He told the court that since that time he had been travelling about the country in search of work, but had been unable to find any.

Maria Barton's defence counsel Mr Whitfield brought several of her lodgers to prove that she had no ale in the house on the day in question. They admitted that she was in the habit of keeping a barrel of ale in her bedroom for her own consumption, but this barrel had been empty for a few days before. As a consequence of having two sons-in-law in custody in Doncaster on a charge of felony, she was unable to buy more. They all swore most positively that she could not have served Winter any beer as the barrel was empty when he was staying in the house. The magistrate Mr Henry Walker Esq., told the court that there had been doubts about the case before hearing the evidence, but now the bench was unanimous in dismissing the case.

If Maria Barton had got away with serving beer in the house without a licence, she was still being watched, by police. A year later she was brought before the magistrates again after being charged to remove a nuisance from the unclean state of the house on Millgate, which had been caused by keeping pigs in the yard. She was found guilty and fined 5s. Regular reporting of such cases in the local newspapers may have added to her fame but the press first referred to her as 'Lady Barton' in a reporting of a case which took place on Monday 13 May 1850.

She was described as 'the now rather elderly Lady Barton' when two young boys named Henry Jones and John Faulkner went to the house on Millgate with a stolen smock frock. Lady Barton offered them 3d for it, in the presence of a man called Charles Shirtcliffe aged 36 who, despite the discrepancy in age, lived with her in the capacity of a 'protector'. He asked the lads if 'they had brought it from anywhere near'. They told him that they had found the smock in a stable at a farm at Loversall near Doncaster, which was about ten miles from Rotherham.

Shirtcliffe commented on the unusual buttons on the smock and he cut them off. Meanwhile the owner of the smock, a man called William Shepherd, had reported the theft. The following day, police enquiries established that the stolen smock had been seen hanging on the washing line at the house on Millgate. Sergeant Hudson charged Lady Barton with the robbery, but she denied all knowledge of it. Shirtcliffe also denied having anything to do with the smock, but when they searched him, several of the buttons were found sewn up in his clothes.

Two days later the young thieves, Jones and Faulkner were brought into the police station and questioned, and they confessed

46

to the robbery and selling the smock to Barton. They agreed to become witnesses for the prosecution. On Monday 20 May all four prisoners was in court where they were found guilty and sent to take their trial at the Rotherham Quarter Sessions. The prisoners were brought before the magistrates on 8 July 1850 and the sensational nature of the woman ensured newspaper reporting widely on 'the trial of Lady Barton'. The house on Millgate was described as being 'notorious for the frequency with which its occupants have figured before the Rotherham magistrates'.

The court was crowded to see this most notorious local character, and when the jury was being selected, only those who had not heard of her previous reputation were chosen. About half the jury were dismissed, as they admitted to having read about her exploits in the newspapers, but as soon as they moved out of court their place was quickly taken by others. The prisoners were defended by Mr Overend who condemned the evidence against them as being based mainly on the evidence of the two young boys, and on the principle that Lady Barton knew that when she bought the smock from the boys she was aware that the article had been stolen.

John Faulkner was the first to give evidence and was described as a 'youth whose appearance presented the most marked characteristics of a regular jailbird'. He stated that:

'I have pleaded guilty today of stealing a smock frock. I, along with Jones, stole it from Loversall near Doncaster. We then went to Mrs Barton's house and I offered her the smock for sale. She was still in bed when we got there and she waited till this man [Shirtcliffe] came in. When he came in, we sold her the smock for 3d and Shirtcliffe was close by. Shortly afterwards he said "I will get up and take the buttons off". Shirtcliffe asked me in a whisper where I had got the smock from. I told him, and spoke low. Shirtcliffe cut the buttons off and told me that it would be alright'.

In cross-examination the boy stated that he had sold the smock to Mrs Barton in the presence of several of the other lodgers in the house. He also admitted to being previously convicted of felony and sacrilege [robbing from churches]. His statement was confirmed by Henry Jones, and the next witness was Sarah Oldham whose version differed from the others as she appeared with a baby in her arms. She told the magistrates that she was now:

'living in the workhouse. I was living at Barton's when Jones and Faulkner came there. I saw Mrs Barton buy the smock off Faulkner and give him 3d for it. Shirtcliffe came in about an hour afterwards, and Barton said to him "see thee Charles, I have bought thee a smock". Faulkner and Jones were present. Shirtcliffe looked at the smock and asked Faulkner if he had brought it from anywhere near. Barton was present and heard what Shirtcliffe said. Faulkner made answer and said "no". He whispered into Shirtcliffe's ear. Shirtcliffe said "then I will cut the buttons off and it will not be owned". On Wednesday Mrs Barton got a Scotch woman, who lodged at her house to wash the smock'.

At this point Oldham tried to say that whilst she had been living in the workhouse an attempt had been made to threaten her, so that she might not give evidence against the prisoners, but she was stopped from speaking as the evidence was said to be inadmissible. She was then cross-examined by Mr Overend who asked her 'where her husband was' and whether she 'had hired the baby' to create sympathy in the court. Oldham indignantly told him that she had no husband and the baby was her own.
He then asked her if she was a 'common woman of the town' [a prostitute] and she told him with dignity 'I have not been so common that it is too late to mend'. Mr Overend replied 'I hope not. I do not wish to press hardly upon you, but you have been a woman in that class of life?' The witness made no reply and the questioned was not asked again. Oldham admitted having been in prison twice for vagrancy and said that she was already in custody when she made this statement. Police Sergeant Hudson next took the stand and told the court that:

'On the 10 May I went to Mrs Barton's house and charged her with buying a drab smock frock, a small bag and a sack off two prisoners that were in custody named Jones and Faulkner. She said she had not bought anything of that sort, and that they had not had anything of the sort with them. I told her that I knew that the smock frock had been hung out in the yard. She then directed me to the smock frock, which I found still hanging in the yard. All the buttons were off except one. She afterwards said that Faulkner and Jones had washed it and hung it in the yard themselves'.

When Mr Overend began his defence of the prisoners there was laughter in court when he referred to Lady Barton as 'this respectable woman'. But he qualified this statement by adding that:

'it might be that person accustomed to fine carpets and fine sofa's supposed that a person who kept a lodging house could not be respectable. But there were persons keeping lodging houses whose character enabled them to be considered respectable'

He then concluded his evidence by stating to the jury that there was not sufficient evidence on which to find the prisoners guilty. The chair asked the jury whether the prisoner and Shirtcliffe were not both so intimately involved with the purchase of the smock, as to make the act of either or both. It did not take long for the jury to find Lady Barton guilty.

Then it was the trial of Charles Shirtcliffe who was described as being 'a middle aged man on the same charge as Barton, whose paramour he had been for some time'. Once again Mr Overend defended the prisoner. Mr Bland gave evidence that when Shirtcliffe was charged with cutting the buttons off the smock which Barton had bought, he denied all knowledge of the smock and said he had never seen one.

On searching him, the missing buttons were found stitched to his trousers and then he said 'Oh I remember that, a man gave me

49

three or four buttons which I stitched to my trousers'. In the evening Mr Bland saw him again and he stated 'Oh yes I remember now, that I did cut some buttons off the smock in the morning, but I did it at the desire of Faulkner and Jones and they gave me the buttons'.

Mr Overend claimed that the smock was not the stolen one, but one that had been made for the prisoner by Mrs Barton herself. Pointing to the disparity of ages between Mrs Barton and Shirtcliffe, he ridiculed the idea of them living together as man and wife. He commented on the fact that much of the evidence was from a young man, who freely admitted being twice imprisoned for vagrancy and sacrilege. His words were wasted however when the jury almost immediately gave a verdict of guilty.

The four prisoners, Barton, Shirtcliffe, Jones and Faulkner were all placed at the bar for sentencing. The chairman told the prisoners

'we looked upon every receiver of stolen goods as worse than the thief, and that if it were not for them, young travelling thieves such as Faulkner and Jones would not have the same temptation to commit the crimes they did'.

The court sentenced Shirtcliffe to be imprisoned in the House of Correction at Wakefield and to be kept to hard labour for 12 months. His paramour Lady Barton received six months with hard labour. Faulkner who had already admitted his previous charges was transported for seven years. To this sentence he replied 'thank you Sir'. Against Jones there were no previous convictions on record, and the court 'having reason to believe that he had assisted the ends of justice by the evidence he had given that day' was sentenced to just three months imprisonment with hard labour.

The next time we hear of Lady Barton was on the evening of Tuesday 3 June 1851 when there was a fire at the house on Millgate. Described in the newspapers as 'a den of profligacy and

50

infamy' it was alleged that the fire at the house was started by the child of some Irish lodgers. The child had set fire to a large quantity of wood shavings that were being used for a bed. The shavings, although damp, were quickly ignited and the room was soon in flames. It was reported that 'the North of England Fire Brigade with their engine quickly attended, followed almost immediately by the Sun engine'. Buckets were used and by the united exertions of the firemen and townspeople, the fire was quickly brought under control without doing much damage.

In lodging houses and brothels fights often broke out and the one belonging to Lady Barton on Millgate was no different. On August 9 1851 there was a stabbing reported at the house when a man called Patrick Masterman was charged with stabbing James Heppenstall. At the time there was much prejudice against Irish people living in the town. The newspaper reported that 'the parties reside in Millgate, which locality swarms with low lodging houses chiefly occupied by Irish'. It seems that on that night there had been a regular riot in the neighbourhood, mainly run by 'the Irish' who turned out armed with pokers, tongs and other weapons they could find.

Heppenstall, who was the son-in-law of Lady Barton, claimed that he took no part in the affray but was looking on quietly from the door of the house on Millgate when Masterman came up and stabbed him on the forehead. He claimed that he had managed to hold onto him until his brother went to his assistance. Constables were called to quell the riot and Patrick Masterman was arrested, and sent to take his trial at the assizes, where he was sentenced to ten years transportation.

Lady Barton, who now after serving her six months prison sentence, once again returned back to the house on Millgate, and continued to frustrate the respectable inhabitants. Conditions inside the houses left a lot to be desired and were described on 25 March 1852 when the Chief Constable Mr Bland continued his vendetta against Lady Barton. Part of his responsibilities were to visit all the lodging houses in the town. On that day he had gone to her brothel/lodging house and found it to be very overcrowded. He found that there were in total there were fifteen persons when she was only registered to have ten and once again she was arrested and brought in front of the magistrates.

Mr Bland told the court that on the ground floor of the house there was a coal cellar. In it, and sleeping on a litter of straw, were two girls who earned their living by prostitution. Also in the room was a man who was sleeping on a chair. He described the stench from the small room, which measured four feet long and three feet wide, and said it was 'intolerable'. When Mr Bland went upstairs he found a man and a woman in one bed, and four other persons in another bed in the same room. In a second bedroom a man and two women were sleeping together in a bed, and the same number in another bed in the same room. Lady Barton was fined 40s and costs.

The sensational way in which the story was reported, gives an indication not only of the lives that people were living in the town at the time, but also to the shocking fact of men and women sleeping in the same bed. The following year in April 1853 she was again fined another 40s and costs for the same offence. It is interesting to note that at the same time a Charles Elliott of Westgate was only fined 20s on a similar charge. On December 24 1853 she was fined £5 and costs for the same offence but but it was reported to be 'of a more aggravated nature'.

By January 1855 the town of Rotherham [or perhaps it was the dogged pursuit of Mr Bland] caused Lady Barton to finally leave the town and move to the village of Whiston. She still rented the house at Millgate and now rented another at Whiston. It was reported that the village constable however, was still watching the house which he visited on 21 January at 1 am. There he found that although the house was unregistered as such, it was clearly being used as a lodging house. In one bedroom he found two beds containing two person each, and a man and a woman sleeping on the floor.

In another room were another two beds again containing two persons each. Once again Lady Barton was arrested and brought before the court at Rotherham. Her old enemy Mr Bland stated that he had frequently cautioned her against keeping lodgers when the house was not registered. Lady Barton denied this saying 'never, never'. When the magistrate Mr J Fullerton asked her if she had anything to say against the charge, she told him that 'if the bench did not wish her to keep lodgers then she would be without'.

The magistrate told her that she was liable to a fine of £5 and when she told him that she had two houses, he told her that she could then be liable to a fine of £10. Thankfully the bench took pity on her on this occasion, and she was ordered to pay 40s and costs or be committed to prison for six weeks.

Then Maria Barton fades out of history and no more is heard of her through the local newspapers. If Lady Barton had been reported as 'elderly' in July 1850 then it is quite possible that she may have died. Whatever fate befell her, there would be little doubt that if she had come to the end of her life, the police authorities and magistrates of Rotherham would have breathed a great sigh of relief.

Chapter Seven: Neglect of Duty by a Rural Constable.

As early as 1840 it had been suggested that a local police force should be established in Rotherham, based on the lines of the Metropolitan Police Force. It was decided that it would be a paid constabulary force which would be trained and organised and placed in the hands of the local magistrates. The magistrates would choose the Chief Constable, appoint other officers and ensure that they would keep the peace. Rural constables, who were paid out of the rates would continue to patrol the villages of the area, but they were judged to be inefficient and inadequate to secure proper order.

The Chief Constable of the time, Mr Bland had the greatest of difficulties in maintaining discipline among these men who were so spread out over the districts. Nevertheless the role of rural constables were very demanding and the men were expected to be on duty all day, every day. Their duties were very demanding and included serving warrants, arresting people and to pass on all information about any crimes to the police force in Rotherham. Sometimes these men were asked to put themselves in great danger, which for the small amount of pay they received was quite daunting.

On 6 January 1848 the constable of Harthill was a man called Joseph Wilkinson. In the village was a public house called the Hope and Anchor which was run by the wife of a farmer called Mrs Holmes. At lunchtime, on that day a party of railway navvies had arrived at her house in a cart along with another eight or ten persons. Three of the men were named Eccles, Billington and Wade and they appeared to be very unruly. They demanded alcohol, but as they appeared to be already inebriated and liable to become worse, Mrs Holmes refused to serve them.

Billington carried a gun and before he had even got out of the cart, he fired the gun into the air before reloading and following his companions into the public house. When Mrs Holmes refused them ale once again, Billington threatened to shoot her if she did not serve them, and as she walked away from him to go into the yard, he discharged the gun after her. The door through which she passed was studded with shot, and she had a miraculous escape.

Billington coolly reloaded the gun with a cap given to him by one of his companions. One of Mrs Holmes servant's, a man called Joseph Webster tried to prevent the man from firing at his mistress again, and told him that his behaviour was 'past a joke'. In reply the navvy told him that he would 'blow his brains out' and instantly pointed the gun at him and pulled the trigger. Thankfully twice the gun misfired until one of the navvies, the man called Eccles, stopped Billington from firing again and the party went outside into the yard.

Mrs Holmes had enough and she sent Webster for the rural constable, John Wilkinson. The three men were now getting belligerent and the situation was only saved when some more people were heard coming up the lane towards the public house. When they heard this, the men hurriedly left. It was later reported that they went to another pub in the neighbouring village of Swallownest, where they were more successful and were served with alcohol.

When Mrs Holmes heard that the navvies were drinking at Swallownest, she sent Joseph Webster to the magistrate Mr Althorpe asking for a warrant for the arrest of Billington for attempted murder. The magistrate complied and the warrant was given to Webster, who was instructed to hand it to PC Wilkinson to execute. Webster went to Harthill, but the constable told him that he could not serve it that day as he had to go to Worksop market. He instructed Webster to take the warrant to the house of a man named Martin Clayton.

He was not a regular constable, but had been sworn in to act as a special constable in cases of riot. But finding that Clayton was not at home, Webster went back to Wilkinson, who then told him to take it to the constable of Wales and ask him to serve it instead. After Webster was unable to locate even that constable, he was forced to go into back to Mrs Holmes and inform her that the warrant could not be served. Two days later, on Thursday 8 January the Rotherham police were made aware of the circumstances that the warrant had not been served, and an enquiry was put in place. It was established that at the time Webster was asking Wilkinson to serve the warrant and he refused, the man Billington lay drunk at a village not a mile away from Swallownest.

As a consequence of the enquiry, PC Joseph Wilkinson was brought before the Chief Constable, Mr Bland and severely reprimanded for his behaviour. When his case was brought before the Watch Committee, they stipulated that he would have to be taken before the magistrates in order that an example be made of him for the benefit of other rural constables. As a consequence Wilkinson appeared before Mr George Wilton Chambers Esq., and Mr Henry Walker Esq., on Monday 24 January 1848 charged with neglect of duty.

Mr Bland described the case for the bench and told them that although the navvies had been drinking at the next village for most of that day, that Billington had now absconded and they had not since been able to apprehend him. Had Wilkinson done his duty, as he ought to have done, the man would have been speedily captured and brought before the magistrates. Wilkinson was asked if he wanted to say anything to the charge, and he stated that he had received the warrant and read it over, but had a particular engagement at Worksop which he could not avoid.

He said that as the offence was committed in the Wales district, that he was justified in sending Webster for the constable there. He had always understood that it was the constable of the place where the offence had been committed, that had to take the responsibility for serving a warrant.
In mitigation, Webster told the magistrates that when anything previously had occurred in that area, he had always gone to

56

Wilkinson who had never objected to act before. One of the magistrates Mr Walker stated that:

'a great injury had arisen to the public in this case; the parties charged with a very grave offence, having through the neglect of the constable, escaped the hands of justice. The county had been put to several pounds expense in endeavouring to discover them, when they might have been apprehended at once by Wilkinson if he had acted properly'.

Mr Walker criticised the negligence of constables of the outlying districts of the town, who he said 'showed too much indifference in the discharge of their duties'. Mr Bland told him that the constables own private business should not be put before the police business that they were paid to undertake. The magistrate told Wilkinson that the warrant should have been executed without delay, as soon as it was placed in his hands. He ordered that Wilkinson pay a fine of £2 and costs, and intimated that in any other similar case brought before the bench, would inflict fines of £5.

This was an enormous fine for Wilkinson to find and it would not have made him any more diligent in his post. His conduct just added to the general dissatisfaction that most local people felt towards the development of a police force for Rotherham. It was not until the Police Act of 1856 which brought in a system of governmental control that the police force that we know today came into being. Regular inspections took place and grants given to more efficient forces resulted in better policing and solving of crimes.

Chapter Eight: Highway Robbery near Kimberworth.

On Monday 29 October 1849 an elderly farmer named Joseph Warris went into the Queens Arms, a public house at Masbrough. He transacted some business with the landlady, Mrs Sarah Hewitt before going through into the main room where he ordered a drink of beer. Sarah was a single young woman who had gained quite a reputation as she took in lodgers at the pub, and had acquired a certain character for 'looseness'. Despite being 72 years of age Joseph had been witnessed on several occasions kissing Sarah Hewitt.

The reason might have been that she had challenged him that if he bought a half a gallon of ale, she would give him a kiss. As might be deduced from his activities with the young landlady, he was a sociable man, and on that Monday night in question he was soon he in conversation with a group of four other men. They were James Badger, and Thomas Makin of the Holmes, and George Straw and John Bagnall of Masbrough. Joseph bought half a gallon of ale which he shared with the men which presumably got him another kiss from Sarah.

The men solicitously asked Warris if he could afford to buy them drinks, and foolishly he showed them several sovereigns that he had in his pocket. Just before 11 pm Joseph's son William called in to the pub to walk his father home. The two men left and started up the hill in the moonlight towards his farm at Kimberworth. As they passed the Masbrough toll-bar, which was situated near to Ferham House, four men hurried past them who seemed to be hiding their faces. Towards the top of the hill there was a small plantation at the side of the road where one of the men, Thomas Makin, appeared to be leaning against the plantation wall as if drunk.

As the two men passed him Makin ran up behind them, and knocked Joseph to the floor telling him 'Warris, I mean to have

58

some of your money from you'. Joseph felt Makin put his hand into his breeches and attempted to take his money. As the men struggled Makin whistled, and the three other men came running towards them. The elderly man's son William made no attempt to help his father, and instead ran away in the direction of Masbrough crying out 'murder'.

The men robbed Joseph of six sovereigns before disappearing into the night. After the men had gone, Joseph managed to get up and he walked back into Rotherham to inform the police of the robbery. He told them that because of the bright moonlight he had recognised the men who had earlier been drinking with him. The following day John Bagnall, James Badger and Thomas Makin were arrested. Makin denied the charge stating that he had left Joseph at the Queens Arms being entertained by Bagnell, who was singing a song for the crowd.

Badger and Bagnall also denied the charge. Badger claimed that Joseph was still in the pub when he left and Bagnall stated that he had stayed long after Joseph had left. On Tuesday George Straw was also arrested and he was taken to the police station at Rotherham, where he too claimed he was innocent. He told Inspector Bland that 'he was innocent of the robbery, but that he would tell all he knew about it'. He swore that he had been near the plantation on the night in question looking for a hare, when he saw the three other prisoners walking towards Kimberworth. When the men started to attack Joseph, he saw the younger Warris run away shouting 'murder'.

When he saw the men robbing the elderly man, he too became frightened and ran back home.
Ignoring their pleas of innocence the four men were brought into court on Thursday 1 November before the magistrate Henry Walker Esq. They were charged with highway robbery, and the violent assault of Joseph Warris. It was reported that the elderly man 'wavered considerably in his cross examinations as to the identity of the four men'. But his evidence was confirmed by his son William who identified seeing the prisoners in the public

59

house with his father. They were all remanded in custody for a week, but only James Badger was given bail.

When the enquiry was re-convened, the pub manager of the Queens Arms, Mr Frith told the court that he remembered the elderly farmer leaving the house about 10.45 pm, and the four prisoners leaving shortly afterwards. He described how he had gone to the door to lock up and watched as Badger, Bagnell and Makin followed Joseph up the road towards the toll-bar. The three men were closely followed by Straw. He told the magistrate that he was puzzled, as it was not the prisoners usual route home. Straw told the court that he was innocent of the robbery, although again confessing that he had been there at the time.

Despite all their statements of innocence, the four prisoners were committed to have their case heard at the assizes. On Friday 9 November 1849 John Bagnall, James Badger, George Makin and Thomas Straw were all removed from Rotherham to York Castle to await their trial. The four men appeared at York assizes on Thursday 13 December in front of Mr Justice Cresswell. Mr Overend defended Badger and Mr Hardy was counsel for Straw and Makin, only Bagnall was undefended.

Mr Hall for the prosecution outlined the case for the jury. He stated that Mr Warris knew Makin very well, and was easily able to recognise him as one of the men who had attacked him on the night of the robbery. The other three he knew only by sight, but he had no doubt about their identity as the men who had stolen £6. The defence tried to imply that Joseph was very intoxicated on the night of the robbery, and therefore he was mistaken in his identity of the four men. Witnesses were also brought to speak of the good character of Makin, Straw and Bagnall.

It did no good however, and it only took the jury ten minutes to declare all four men guilty of the charge. Mr Justice Cresswell told the prisoners that the uncalled for violence they had used on the elderly man, who had shown them nothing but kindness, had appalled him. He was determined to make an example of them therefore as he sentenced them to be transported over the seas for a period of seven years each.

Transportation was seen at the time as an alternative to incarceration within the prison system. Prisoners being condemned for transportation would firstly serve some part of their sentence in local gaols such as Wakefield or York in solitary confinement. Then the Secretary of State would give a date for transportation and they might be moved to one of the hulks, which were old Navy ships, no longer fit for purpose. Only from there did they go to new South Wales to serve out the rest of their sentence. One thing is for sure, the four men from Rotherham had seven years to regret their actions on the road to Kimberworth in October of 1849.

Chapter Nine: 'One of the Worst Families in Rotherham'.

In 1851 there was a most notorious family that lived in town called the Tattersall's. Both mother and father were well known to the police authorities for their drunkenness, and it was said that their sons John aged 20 and William aged 18 had inherited their parents bad habits. They also had a younger brother called George who was only 14, but showed all the early signs of following in the family footsteps. On Monday 31 March the family was all drinking in the Swan Inn with several others. The group included a stove grate fitter called George Mortomley who lived at Masbrough.

At about 10.30 pm he was invited back to the Tattersall's house on Westgate by Mrs Tattersall. At first she went out to get some more beer, but due to the late hour she was unsuccessful. Mortemley stated that he would be able to find somewhere and quickly returned back with half a gallon of beer from a nearby beer house called Jackson's, which they all drank together. At this point young George Tattersall returned home and asked for some supper before going to bed. His mother told him that if he did not 'sit down and hold your noise, I will knock you down'. As is inevitable with drinking, an argument broke out between the mother and father which was overheard by their older sons William and John who rented the house next door.

The two men came into their parents house and Mortemley, who had taken no part in the argument, got up to leave. He was walking down the lane towards his own house, when he heard himself being pursued by all three Tattersall brothers. The next thing he knew he was being thrown to the ground. The youngest son George wielded a poker and hit Mortemley three times over the head with it, as the victim tried to protect himself with his arms, which as a result, were bruised and bleeding.

62

The injured man somehow got to his feet and backed towards a gas light, but the two men and the boy continued beating him. To his horror Mortemley saw that William had something bright in his hand, just before he told him 'I'll give you some of this' as he felt a vicious cut across his nose. Mortemley shouted 'murder, murder' at the top of his voice, which fortunately was heard by Police Constable Timms. As the officer approached the men ran off, and he found Mortemley bleeding profusely from his head wounds and the cut on his nose.

Following the man's statement PC Timms arrested William, John and George Tattersall and they were taken to the police cells and searched. William denied having a knife in his possession and none was found on him. John denied the charge and told the arresting officer that George Mortomley had started the fight in the first place. He claimed that the man had brought some ale to the house, and shortly afterwards he had nearly killed their mother before abusing young George Tattersall. When PC Timms returned back to the place where the attack had taken place, he found a clasp knife with blood on the blade.

William, George and John Tattersall appeared in court the following day before the magistrate Mr H Walker Esq., A witness called Elizabeth Stevenson confirmed the latter part of Mortemley's statement as she had seen the attack made on him. The three prisoners were all found guilty, and were sent to take their trial at the next assizes. All three applied for bail, but it was only granted in the case of young George and John.

As was usual, the assize judge, Mr Justice Williams discussed all the cases with the Grand Jury before the trial commenced in July 1851. He told them that from the depositions it would seem that William Tattersall was the only person to use a knife. He said that if they agreed, then the question they had to consider was how far the other two were responsible for his having done so. He told them that:

'if several persons engage in assaulting another man, they are all answerable for the acts of each other. Therefore if you think there is evidence of 'common purpose' then you must find a true bill against all three prisoners. But if you find there was no 'common purpose', and that William alone was intending grievous bodily harm, you must find a true bill again that prisoner alone and throw out the bills against the other two'.

The Grand Jury agreed and the case against John and George Tattersall was dismissed.

William Tattersall appeared at the York assizes on Tuesday 16 July 1851 before Mr Justice Platt, charged with attempted murder. The prosecutor, Mr Overend described the row which had developed between the Tattersall's who he described as 'one of the worst families in the town'. PC Timms described how he had gone to arrest William and he found both the mother and father to be in a very drunken state. William told him that Mortemley had insulted his mother and was beating up his young brother George when William and John entered the house.

He admitted that they had bundled Mortemley out of the house roughly, but he denied having or using a knife. PC Timms told the court that he had found the clasp knife, which had been identified as one belonging to the victim, George Mortomley. He thought that the knife had probably dropped through a hole in his pocket during the struggle. The Constable deduced that the prisoner had probably picked it up and used it.

Then there occurred a complete twist in the trial which sometime happens. Far from being a member of the worst family in Rotherham, witnesses now gave evidence that William had tried very hard to improve himself and distance himself from the rest of his family. The witness Elizabeth Stevenson, who had seen the prisoners attack Mortemley, stated that William had an irreproachable character, and she blamed the incident on the prisoners 'intemperate parents'. Several other witnesses also

64

claimed that William, despite his misfortune in his parentage, had 'raised himself above them'.

PC Timms also confirmed that on the night in question, both parents were very drunk and William claimed that they were all inebriated before Mortemley was driven out of the house. The defence suggested that the victim had actually taken out his own knife out to defend himself, and in the scuffle had cut himself on the nose. Even the judge himself seemed to defend William. He told the jury that great allowances had to be made for the prisoner, who hearing the attack from next door:

'found George Mortemley with his parents under disgraceful circumstances and with the assistance of his brothers, forcibly ejected him from the house. In judging this case you must not allow your feelings of indignation at the conduct of those involved, or the sympathy for the victim, to lead you to return a verdict in opposition to the evidence. The only question which you have to ask yourselves was did the prisoner inflict the wound with intent to do serious bodily harm'

The jury after consulting together for a few moments found William Tattersall not guilty on the charge of attempted murder, but guilty of unlawful wounding. The judge agreed and because the prisoner had already spent three months in prison, he sentenced William to just one month in York Castle prison. The judge directed the governor, who had attended the court, to ensure that during his confinement the prisoner was to be kept from the 'bad company of other prisoners'.

Before William left the dock, the judge expressed a hope that this would prove to him to be a lesson in life and under no circumstance was he to resort again to the use of the knife. No doubt William was greatly relieved as he returned to the bosom of his dubious family.

Chapter Ten: Attempted Murder at Brinsworth Bar

As we have already seen the condition of the some of the roads around Rotherham were so poor that turn pike trusts were set up to repair them and toll booths established. As we have also seen these booths were ripe for criminals to attack and such a one was at Brinsworth. On the morning of Friday 19 November 1852 a murderous assault took place on the keeper of the Brinsworth toll bar, a man called Robert Hansley. The bar was on the main Sheffield to Bawtry Road and situated about two miles from the centre of the town itself. The position of the toll bar was of some concern to the keeper, as it was in a lonely, isolated setting and there were no houses within a half mile in either direction.

This combined with the fact that Robert Hansley and his wife were in their sixties made them an easy target. Nevertheless despite his age Hansley was aware of the danger, and subsequently kept a pistol ready and loaded which he placed on the mantelpiece in the lower room at the bar. He also kept a ferocious dog which he was convinced would fly at anyone attempting to break into the place, and rip them to pieces. Hansley's reputation and bravery were well known in the district, as he had frequently boasted that if anyone attempted to break into his toll bar, he would shoot the first man that entered.

All the money that was collected was paid over every month to the bank in Rotherham. Hansley was also aware that any thieves breaking in when the money was due to be paid into the bank, would have got a substantial amount of money. Early that morning at 1.15 am the toll gate keeper was awoken by cry of 'gate' and he looked out of the window where he saw a man sitting on an ass on the road. Hansley was confused, because there were two posts at the side of the bar which were sufficiently wide to allow a man and an ass to get through easily at no cost. He shouted down to the man to pass through the posts, but the man retorted that the ass was shy, and would not pass through such a little opening.

No doubt cursing the erstwhile traveller for disturbing him, Hansley got up and dressed to let the man through the gate. The man asked him how much the toll would be and he told him three half pence. The man dismounted before reaching into his pocket saying that he would need change for 6d. That was when a second man who had been crouching down at the side of the toll house, sprang up and hit Hansley over the head with a hedge stick.

The man with the ass also landed some heavy blows on the elderly man, who was now on the floor and curled up in a ball trying to protect himself. Inside the toll house Mrs Hansley let go the fierce dog telling him to attack the men outside. Sadly it was reported that:

'singularly enough the ferocious disposition of the animal seemed entirely to have disappeared, and the dog simply frisked about the men as if enjoying the scene'.

Hansley meanwhile managed to get away from the two men and rushed back into the lower room of the toll house. He grabbed the loaded pistol and was in the act of pointing it at the two intruders, who had followed him inside, when one of them knocked it out of his hand. They then proceeded to beat him savagely once again with the hedge stick and an iron poker taken from the fireplace. Mrs Hansley screamed out 'murder' at the top of her voice, but her husband was beaten almost insensible as he lay on the floor covered in blood.

The two men then turned their attention to the woman. Grabbing her from behind and holding a knife to her throat, they used the most awful threats of what they would do to her if she did not hand over all the money in the house. As it happened the money had just been paid in to the bank a few days earlier and she told them this, but they did not believe her. One of them stayed with the injured man, whilst the other accompanied her to the upper rooms. There they ransacked all the drawers and cupboards searching for any valuables or cash.

Despite their frantic search the men only found Hansley's silver watch, some plated spoons which they mistook for silver, two silk handkerchiefs and about £4. 10s in money. So threatening were the men towards her, that Mrs Hansley even handed over the few half pennies she had in her apron pocket. As they left the toll house they told the elderly couple to go back to bed, and warned them that if they tried to attract any help before 4 am they would returned and murder them both. The two men then left locking the bedroom door and the back door, taking the keys with them.

No one else passed the gate until 6 am when a man called Daniel Jenkinson was passing on his way to Sheffield. Mrs Hansley opened the bedroom window and shouted down to him and told him that herself and her husband had been locked in the upstairs room following a robbery. Jenkinson managed to get a ladder and entering the house he prise open the bedroom door, setting the elderly couple free. Dr Hardwicke the surgeon from Rotherham was called to attend to Hansley and he arrived almost immediately.

Tending to the keeper, he found four very contused wounds on his head, two on his back, one on the right side and another on the forehead. His left shoulders and the upper parts of his arms where he had tried to defend himself, were also very much bruised. The man was sent into hospital where his condition was still very precarious for a day or so after the attack. It was reported that it was strongly suspected that if inflammation set in, then his recovery would be impossible. Dr Hardwicke had also informed the Rotherham police, and in daylight they could easily see the evidence of the vicious nature of the attack.

On the outside doorstep and underneath the window, where the first attack had taken place, were many spattered bloodstains. Inside was even worse, with the floor, walls, furniture, ceiling and clothes all covered with the keeper's blood. A description of the

68

two men was given to the Chief Constable, and posters giving the description of the men were circulated throughout Rotherham. It was said that both men were aged between 22 and 25 years of age, and had light features and a clear faces. They were of middle stature, wearing blue and white 'slops' and caps. [slops were the cheaper kind of home made clothing].

A close search was made of the neighbourhood and a reward of £150 was offered for the capture and conviction of the two robbers. Police enquiries quickly established that prior to the robbery, the same two men had made their way to Rotherham, entering the town in the early hours of Thursday morning. Their rough appearance had alerted the police and they had been questioned, but claimed that they were just navvies coming to the town in search for work. They gave their names as Thomas Jackson and William Thompson.

Thankfully a close eye had been kept on the two men by the Rotherham police, and as a consequence they had been seen going in the direction of Brinsworth by Police Constable Timms in the early hours on the morning of the robbery. Another witness saw them at Canklow Mills, within a mile of the bar. Timms description, as well as that given by Mrs Hansley, convinced the local police that these were the same two men who had committed the robbery. Police enquiries revealed that the reason for threatening the couple before locking them in, was because the two men intended to rob another toll bar at Wickersley.

They found that when the robbers got to Brecks farm they went into a stable and stole a horse. One of the men was riding the horse as he approached the Wickersley toll bar and once again shouted for the keeper to let them through, whilst the second man stayed hidden. As before, the toll bar keeper told him to pass through the posts, but when he refused the toll keeper was suspicious. The fact that the man wanting to pass the toll bar was wearing poor clothing, and that he was riding a horse with no saddle or bridle, made the keeper think that 'mischief was intended'.

69

Just then a waggon appeared on the road, and the toll keeper had no option but to let the two vehicles through. He noted that the man had looked very disgruntled as he paid the toll. The police were convinced that if the waggon had not appeared, the toll bar keeper would also have been attacked and robbed. The horse that had been used in the attempted robbery, was later found grazing in a field a half mile from the bar. It was re-claimed by the farmer from whose stable it had been taken.

Although only one man was seen, there was little doubt in the mind of the Rotherham police that these were the same two men who had been stopped in Rotherham the day before who had perpetrated both robberies. This belief was solidified when a witness came forward who had seen the two men approaching Wickersley, and they were later seen at Bramley. What the Rotherham Chief Constable found out from a report that on the previous Tuesday the two men had been in the custody of the Newark police charged with vagrancy, but had been discharged by the magistrates on promising to leave the town. Instead of leaving they had committed a similar robbery at the Debdale Mill toll house on the Newark to Worksop Road.

Their method of operation was the same in all three cases, where one man would decoy the keeper out of the house whilst another, who was concealed, attacked the keeper as he came outside. The report stated that they had proceeded to plunder the Debdale toll house and on this occasion only found £2. After committing this robbery which had given them so little return, they then made their way to Rotherham. The Chief Constable was furious as he felt that if the Newark police had been quicker to circulate the report of the theft at the Debdale Mill bar, an arrest would have been made when the two men had entered Rotherham in the first instant. Instead, by the time the news had come to the town, the two men had disappeared and an intensive search for them was undertaken.

At this time it was strongly suspected that the two men were notorious characters named George Curtis and George Woodcock both from Tickhill near Doncaster. A month later the Chief Constable Mr Bland read a report to say that on 18 December 1852 Woodcock had been arrested on a charged of burglary at Eckington. He was, at that time, imprisoned at Chester City Gaol. The toll bar keeper's wife, Mrs Hansley was taken to Chester to see the prisoner, but she was unable to identify him positively.

It was reported at the time that 'it was hoped that before the man's term of imprisonment had finished, that Mr Hansley would be in a better state of health and he might be able to identify the man'. Sadly by the beginning of the following year it was recorded that Mr Hansley:

'has become quite idiotic and imbecilic, arising in great measure from the injuries he received in the struggle with the two villains'.

However this report must have been exaggerated, because he certainly recovered, enough around fourteen months later to identify the other suspect in the toll bar robbery. By February 1854 George Woodcock had served his sentence at Chester and had been discharged from prison. But Mr and Mrs Hansley were asked to identify another possible suspect. On Thursday 20 February 1854 Sergeant Astwood from the Doncaster police arranged for Mr and Mrs Hansley to see George Curtis at the Morpas toll bar at Tickhill.

Sergeant Astwood told the couple that he had reason to believe from information he had received that Curtis, would pass the toll bar there. The couple were still inside the toll house when Sergeant Astwood met Curtis on the road outside and took him towards the toll house, telling him that two persons wished to see him following a robbery at Brinsworth. Almost immediately after casting eyes on him, the elderly couple identified him as the man who had committed the robbery.

George Curtis was arrested and taken into custody at Doncaster and he gave details that he was the son of a farmer of Tickhill, he was aged 23, and gave his address as Blyth Cottage, Tickhill. When Curtis was brought before the magistrates at the Guild Hall at Doncaster the next day, two representatives of the Sheffield to Bawtry Road Trustees called Messrs Hoyle and Marsh attended. Curtis was found guilty of all the toll bar robberies, and sent to take his trial at the next York assizes.

George Woodcock by this time was serving yet another prison sentence at the Derby House of Correction for a burglary he had committed. He was known to have a violent nature and had already committed a vicious attack on one of the turnkey's at the gaol. Once again Sergeant Astwood and Mr and Mrs Hansley were taken to Derby Gaol, but they were unable to identify the man positively as one of the robbers. On Monday 13 March 1854 George Curtis was brought before the judge, Mr Baron Platt charged with the burglary at the Brinsworth toll bar.

He was also charged with the theft of the silver watch, almost £5 in money and three plated spoons the property of Mr Robert Hansley. The toll keeper told the court that he recognised the prisoner easily, as the two men had remained in the house for a full half an hour during the robbery. During that time they wore no masks and there were two candles burning. Therefore Mr Hansley had plenty of time to watch Curtis and was very confident that he had identified him positively. He told the court that he had recognised him whilst he was still on the road outside the toll bar at Tickhill, even before he had been approached by Sergeant Astwood.

Mr Overend who defended George Curtis, claimed that Mr and Mrs Hansley were wrong in their identification, and there was simply no evidence that the prisoner had taken or tried to sell any of the stolen goods. He claimed that the length of time since the attack, and the old age of the victims had rendered their evidence as worse than useless, and therefore it was impossible for them to speak with any certainty. He stated that on the morning of the

72

attack the elderly couple were still in such a state of shock, that they both told Mr Bland that they would be unable to identify the men.

Mr Bland gave evidence that on the morning of the robbery he had taken down the exact words of the elderly couple. Although Mrs Hansley had given a good description, it was only Mr Hansley that had stated that he didn't think he would be able to describe the men. However he had remembered that one of them had deformed front teeth, which was clearly visible with George Curtis. Mr Bland then read out that the description he had taken down from Mrs Hansley statement, which fitted the prisoner exactly.

After hearing all the evidence the jury found George Curtis guilty of the violent attack on the elderly couple, and the judge agreed. As he told the jury 'you have not rashly come to the conclusion that you have pronounced, and I could not say that it was wrong'. Addressing the prisoner he pronounced the sentence of death, and as the prisoner stood holding the rails of the dock, he shouted

'I am as innocent as these rails. I know nothing about the affair. I hope that God Almighty will strike me dead if I do'.

The judge told him that 'the outrage of which you have been convicted was one of so cowardly and ruffianly a character, that the judgement of the court was that the sentence of death will be recorded'. Curtis was then removed out of the docks and into the cells below.

Thankfully George Curtis did not hang, as his sentence was commuted to transportation for life. He was one of 250 convicts who joined the ship 'William Hammond on 3 January 1856 bound for Western Australia. Interestingly George Woodcock also had his sentence changed to transportation for the burglary for which he had been sentenced. He went out with 270 convicts on the ship the 'Nile' on 18 September 1857 also bound for Western Australia. Although there is no evidence, it is interesting to

73

speculate, whether the two men meet up on those distant shores so far away from their home town of Tickhill?

Chapter Eleven: 'If I cant have you, then no one will'.

On Wednesday 27 December 1854, a very pretty young girl called Harriet Ardron aged 21, was on the point of being married. The banns had been called at the local church at Thorpe Hesley, and she was busy planning her wedding. Because of her beauty she had several young men interested in her, but had rejected them all for the man she chose to be her fiancé, William Anstone. Harriet lived with her father William Ardron who was described as 'a farmer in humble circumstances', and she was the eldest of five children.

About 7 pm her father decided that he would go out, leaving his daughter seated near to the fire doing some needlework. Half an hour later Harriet was seen by her uncle, Thomas Ardron leaving the house on her way to visit a friend. She was only thirty yards away from the house where her friend Mary Pilley lived, when she was met in the lane by a young man called Daniel Hawksworth.
He was a miner from Chapeltown, near Sheffield, aged 23 years who had been one of her previous suitors, and he long held hopes to make her his wife.

He was also an acquaintance of her present fiancé and there was little doubt that he was jealous of the man who had won her heart. The couple talked together for a while and although Harriet could see that Daniel was getting rather agitated, she felt no alarm. At first they were chatting about mutual acquaintances, before he asked her why she had rejected him. Harriet explained carefully trying not to antagonise him, but she noted that he began to talk more wildly. Finally he said to her 'if I cant have you then no one will'. She saw him reaching into his pocket and to her horror he pulled out a pistol, before threatening to shoot her if she walked away from him.

She started to back away from him in fear, but only thirty yards away from the safety of her father's house, according to his own confession 'he shot her down'. Constable Richard Smith, who lived in the village heard the shot and he ran to the scene. There he saw the body of the young girl lying in the lane and three men stood watching the young woman scream 'as if they were stupefied'. Very quickly a crowd began to gather, and so when Smith enquired 'who had done this?' Daniel calmly replied 'its me that's done it'.

Smith, with the assistance of a man called John Burgin, carried the poor girl back to her father's house and ordered Daniel to march beside them. Reaching the house, he placed Daniel in a chair and told him to 'stay there' until help arrived in the form of Constable William Richardson. All the time Daniel was in the chair he seemed unable to take his eyes off the girl, as if he couldn't believe what he had done. Daniel was taken to Rotherham and a surgeon Mr Stone from Wentworth, was called to attend to Harriet. He found that the shot had entered just below the ribs on the left side and passed into her bowels.

He noted that she also had another wound in her side, just above the hip. The surgeon knew that there was little chance of her recovery and despite his best attentions, Harriet Ardron lingered in great agony until she died at 6.30 pm on the following evening. It would seem that she too could not believe the events which had overtaken her, as before she died she asked a neighbour, Hannah Burgin 'Why did he do this to me?" She admitted to her that 'I have been a little giddy and wild, but I never did him any harm in his life'.

Harriet also told her neighbour that he had pleaded with her to keep company with him again, and said that 'if she would not go with him, she should not go with anyone else'. Every effort had been made to take a dying deposition from the girl, which could only be done in the presence of a local magistrate and his clerk, but she died before such a testimony could be taken. Daniel arrived at the police station at Rotherham accompanied by PC

76

Richardson and he was arrested on a charge of attempted murder. When asked if he had anything to say in his defence, Daniel replied 'I have shot her and I am very sorry'.

Richardson asked him why he had done it, but Daniel gave no reply. The day after he confessed to Inspector Handley that prior to the shooting, he had been talking to the deceased girl about her fiancé William Anstone. Daniel had told Harriet that her fiancé was unworthy of her. Harriet retaliated that 'she had heard enough' and she went to leave him. He admitted that was when he told her that if she went away 'I would blow her wing off' and that was when he shot her.

An inquest was held at the Red Lion at Thorpe Hesley on Saturday 31 December 1854. The Coroner opened the inquest and told the jury that before her death, Harriet had made several statements to other people during her last few hours. Unfortunately as none of them had been recorded officially they were not allowed to be admitted as evidence. Daniel was brought into the room where he was described as 'being very young-looking and slightly made, with intelligent features'. The first witness was Daniel's brother William.

He told the jury that his brother had bought the gun that very day, and that they had been shooting small birds with it. In answer to a question from the Coroner, William stated that prior to death of the girl, Daniel had been sober. The two men John Milnes and George Senior who had been passing at the time of the attack on Harriet, described how they had seen a flash and watched as the girl fell to the floor. They both witnessed Daniel hiding the gun in a nearby house before returning back to the body.

A storekeeper at the shop of Messrs Gibson of Chapeltown gave evidence that Daniel had purchased the gun in order to 'shoot birds with'. Surgeon, Mr Stone told the Coroner that he completed the post mortem with his brother Mr Erasmus Stone, and they found an effusion of blood in the deceased woman's pelvis. He said that death was from inflammation and peritonitis caused by the gun shot wound. Daniel's defence had now changed and he told the inquest that 'he had not shot at her deliberately, but that she had run in front of the gun as he was firing it into the air'.

Whilst he made this statement it was reported that the prisoner appeared to be very distraught. The Coroner admitted that taking everything into consideration, it was 'the worst case he had to bring before a jury in terms of its callousness'. Despite sympathy for his youthful appearance, after only an hours consideration the jury found him guilty of manslaughter and he was sent to take his trial.

On Thursday 8 March, Mr Justice Cresswell told the Grand Jury at the Leeds assizes that he had little doubt on what the outcome of the trial should be. He stated that he had read the depositions and had come to the conclusion that this case was simply one of carelessness on the part of the young man.

So when Daniel Hawksworth was brought to trial at the assizes at Leeds on Thursday 15 March 1855 the judges decision made the outcome a foregone conclusion. In the closing argument the prosecution Mr Pickering, told the jury, that if they believed that the prisoner had deliberately fired the gun, then he would be guilty of murder. However if they thought the gun had gone off accidentally, then it would be a case of manslaughter. Mr Overend, Daniel's defence counsel claimed several reasons why his client should be discharged.

He reminded the jury that no clear motive had been assigned to the case, and also that Daniel had made no attempt to leave the scene after the gun had gone off. He stated that there was simply no evidence to show that the prisoner had intended to shoot the girl, other than her own statement to the neighbour. Therefore all the facts indicated clearly that the prisoner had shot the girl by accident and the only charge that he was guilty of was 'the reckless and careless handling of a gun'.

After hearing all the evidence the jury found him guilty of manslaughter. They then asked the judge for clemency for the prisoner due to his young age. Daniel who had barely lifted his head throughout the trial made no response. The judge concurred that he had not meant to shoot the girl, but stated that 'he had nevertheless used a dangerous weapon, and must be punished as a warning to others'. Sentence was deferred to the following day, when Daniel Hawksworth was sent to prison for six months.

The fact that whether or not Daniel had intended to shoot Harriet was minimised during the trial, but nevertheless the statements he made, had condemned him. The fact that he had robbed a young girl and her fiancé of a life together, and only served a six month sentence seems clearly unfair. In those days very little attention was paid at this time to a prisoners sanity as he committed the crime. I would suggest that the fascination with which he watched her dying in her fathers house, perhaps may suggest some form of mental disturbance at the very least.

Chapter Twelve: Highway Robbery in Wentworth Park.

In 1855 Messrs Dawes and Company had extensive iron works in, and around the town of Rotherham, and at Milton and Elsecar. They had a large workforce including two elderly men called Robert Myers and Charles Berry. Their specific task amongst other duties, was to go to the Sheffield and Rotherham Bank in the town centre, and pick up the money needed to pay the men their weekly wages. Berry was employed the rest of the week as a storekeeper, and Myers, who was a large man, was employed as a groom at the works.

They were provided with a dog cart for the five mile journey to pick up the wages and were regularly seen on a Saturday morning going backwards and forwards through Greasbrough and Wentworth Park, the seat of Earl Fitzwilliam. A few weeks previously the groom had undertaken the task on his own, on horseback carrying two loaded pistols, but for some time there had been concerns about his safety and Messrs Dawes and Company felt that it would be safer to send two men. They had felt that no one would attack two men in broad daylight.

On Saturday 5 May 1855 the men left the works at 11 am to collect the sum of £800 from the bank. The bag of money containing equal portions of gold and £5 bank notes was placed at the bottom of the cart and covered with a rug. The Earl's carriageway extended to the village of Greasbrough, and about half way along between the village and Wentworth House is a lodge. About 400 yards beyond this lodge is a small round plantation, on the right hand side of the carriage way.

On their journey back, the men had reached this plantation about 12 pm when Myers and Berry saw two men emerge from the plantation adjacent to the carriage way. One man, who was carrying a life preserver, seized the horses head and pulled the cart to a halt. The other brandished a pistol and demanded the money. Both men looked strong and powerfully built, one was tall and the other was of average size. One of the robbers held onto the pony's reins whilst the other, still holding the pistol dragged Myers down from the cart, and declared that he would blow the old man's brains out. They both threatened the men that if they didn't give up the money they would die.

The two elderly men declared bravely that they had no money with them, but their errand was too well known. One of the attackers told them 'you have, if you don't deliver it up, we will blow your brains out directly'. The two robbers left the two elderly men in no doubt that they knew about their errand, and also the fact that they would be carrying a large amount of money with them. The man holding the life preserver then got into the cart where he struck Berry two heavy blows, before proceeded to ransack the contents.

Bravely Berry stood upon the rug laid on the floor of the cart and denied that they had any money with them. The taller robber smashed open a box in the cart and dragged out the cushions and some other articles, but they did not see the money underneath the old carpet. Several times he pulled back a corner of the rug, but did not spot the bag underneath. Bravely Berry made no resistance, but kept his feet firmly planted on the rug.

The robber then hit him over the head twice and demanded the money and once again he told him that there was no money. In disgust the man jumped out, little suspecting that he had just missed finding £800. Myers was thrown roughly down on the floor and he struggled with the robber for a few minutes, before the man put the pistol to his throat and repeated the threat to blow out his brains if he did not give up the money. Myers shouted out 'murder, murder' at the top of his voice.

The robber tore open Myers' trousers and roughly dragged open his pockets, where he found a tin box with three half crowns in change and some keys. There was also a lambskin tobacco pouch filled with some tobacco. Holding up the pouch, the man shouted to his companion that he had found the money. The tobacco pouch being soft to the touch, looked like it contained paper bills. Without looking inside and just assuming that the pouch contained the wages they wanted, the two men ran off.

When they found themselves alone, Berry picked up the reins and even though he was bleeding himself, he told the injured man on the ground that he would fetch medical help for him. Blood was still running down Myers face and he looked a dreadful sight. He urged the animal towards Wentworth House. But Myers, seeing that Berry was going for assistance, got up from the floor and determinedly followed the two robbers for a while, hoping to keep them in sight for when help arrived. He saw them pause at a bridge which led across a brook leading towards Masbrough, and at that point he felt it more prudent to return.

On his way towards Wentworth house he was met by the dog cart now being driven by a porter called Wadsworth, with another man. They both helped the injured man into the cart, but being determined to see which way the two robbers had gone Myers urged them to drive towards where the two robbers had last been seen. They arrived at the bridge but could not find any trace of them. Berry meanwhile had taken the money out of the dog cart and handed the reins to the porter to bring back his injured friend. Still bleeding he then he went to the office of Mr Moore the Earl's head saddler and gave information of the attack to him.

He passed him the bag containing the money, before going to the house of surgeon Mr Stone of Wentworth and begging him to return with him to attend to his companions wounds. The surgeon quickly headed for Wentworth House and attended to both Myers and Berry. He examined Myers and found two very severe wounds in the poor man's head, one on the top and the other on the left hand side. Berry's wounds were more superficial. Mr Moore delivered the money bag to Messrs Dawes and Company's ironworks and told them that the two employers had acted with the utmost bravery, despite the threats of violence. A description of the two men was given to Airey the Constable of Wentworth which was quickly circulated.

Within hours, news of the attack it was being discussed in the town of Rotherham and a search was carried out to try to find the two robbers. The frustration of the people of the town for the non arrest of the robbers resulted in many theories. Despite Berry and Myer's undoubted bravery, the way they had acted was questioned as to why the two robbers had so successfully escaped. It was thought that if Berry had given news of the attack at Mr Honess's house, the stud groom to the Earl who lived nearest, several workmen were on the premises and they might have given chase on horseback and capturing the robbers more quickly.

Throughout the attack the two men had shouted 'murder' and some people thought that it was surprising that their shouts had not attracted any more attention. Mr Horniss himself was only about 200 yards away from the carriageway. There had been a number of workmen in and around the estate grounds, who should have heard their cries. Later it was deduced that the strength of the wind that was blowing at the time had silenced the men's shouts and prevented others from coming to their rescue. Berry later said that he had seen two boys who seemed to be watching the attack from the vicinity of Mr Horniss's house.

Myers also stated that he could see a woman approaching from the same direction. She appeared to stop in her tracks as she saw the struggle, but made no effort to attract any help. Finally on May 12 it was announced that two men had finally been arrested and were in custody charged with the robbery. It was said that the men had been captured mainly by the efforts of Superintendent Green of the Sheffield Police force. One was a man called James Ashton aged 34 who had been arrested at the Railway Tavern in Barnsley. He was said to be a local man who travelled over the area with a grinding wheel seeking knives and other implements to grind.

The other man, a weaver from Barnsley called James Derby aged 26, was arrested in Wentworth village also by Superintendent Green. The two men were taken before the magistrate Mr T Taylor at Barnsley on Friday 11 May and placed in the lobby of the Barnsley Court house where they were identified by Myers and Berry. Without any hesitation they were pointed out from the several other men paraded before them. The men were brought into the Rotherham courthouse the following Monday where James Ashton was described as a 'dark complexioned man'. The newspapers proclaimed that 'the case had been of such considerable interest, that there was a large concourse of people assembled in the vicinity of the Court House waiting to see the two men arrive'.

Many in the crowd were from the towns of Sheffield and Rotherham and more from the village of Wentworth itself. Solicitor Mr Whitfield appeared on behalf of Dawes and Company and Mr Hamer defended the prisoners. Charles Berry was the first witness and he told the court:

'I have been in the employ of Messrs Dawes for five years. On the fifth instant I went to Rotherham in company with Robert Myers, for money to pay the wages with. We went through Wentworth Park and arrived in Rotherham about twelve o'clock. We left the bank about half past twelve and I put the letter bag containing the money in the bottom of the dog cart inside the foot mat. On returning from the bank, Mr John Harrison passed us at a place called Greasbrough Hill. Near the Wentworth Lodge, there is a slight hill to ascend, and a plantation on the right hand side.

Two men rushed out of there and walked a few paces towards us. One walked up to the pony and the other stood on the other side. They both together said 'deliver your money' and the man on my right hand side held a pistol and the other held something bright, but I could not tell whether it was a pistol or not. They demanded our money several times while they were holding the pony. I said I had got no money.

The man on the right hand side let go of the pony and came into the dog cart where I was seated. He turned the foot mat up and not finding anything, left my side and went to Myers side and pulled him out of the dog cart. When he had done this, the other one came to the cart where Myers had been sitting and opened the driving box lid. The other man and Myers were still struggling together. I looked towards the lodge and shouted 'murder'. I was standing up in the cart. Derby came up to me and struck me over the head with what seemed to be a cane handle. I staggered but I did not fall. He struck me with the instrument twice and my head was cut and bled a good deal.

After he struck me, he left the cart and I drove towards the lodge leaving Myers. Blood was running out of my hat. I turned into the main road and asked a person to get into the car with me and then I drove to Wentworth House. The money was all safe in the bag. When I was struck I was standing on the rug under which the money was. I gave information of the robbery at Wentworth House. I am quite certain the two prisoners are the men. I have no doubt whatever'

Cross examined by Mr Hamer, he told him that he was alarmed when the man holding the pistol pointed it at him. Berry then continued with his statement:

'The next time I saw both men was last Friday week. There were two other men with them. The two other men were without anything on their heads. Neither of them were dressed like the prisoners. I was the first who went in to look at them that day. I did not hesitate in pointing out Derby. I had not a doubt that he was the man when I saw his features. I will take it upon myself to say that the tall man is one of those that attacked us. The little one, Ashton presented the pistol at me and the big one struck me. The little one let go of the reins and came to the side of the dog cart and pulled the mat up'

Robert Myers corroborated the evidence and in addition he said:

85

'they both had pistols. The lesser man, who was on Berry's side came round to me and demanded my money. I said we have none and he then pulled me out of the cart. I had a small box in my right pocket and 7s 6d and three keys in the same pocket. The lesser man pulled my pocket off and split my trousers and took all away. I had a tobacco pouch in my left hand waistcoat pocket. He then threw me down on the ground and kneeled upon me and presented a pistol at my head. He said 'I will blow your brains out and cut your throat into the bargain, if you don't deliver up'.

I said I will deliver up if you keep that thing [meaning the pistol] off my head. I was very much alarmed. After the struggle, the bigger man went across the park taking my money towards a road leading to a wood, and the lesser man followed. I ran after them about 150 to 200 yards and they halted on seeing me follow them. I could not see anyone about except a woman who was a good way off. I am quite certain the prisoners are the men.

He too was cross examined by Mr Harmer and he told him:

'I was very much alarmed when they seized the pony. I had never seen either man before that time to my knowledge. It was the little one that got me down. The big one was on the other side of the cart. They have not the same dress on now as they had when they attacked us. I will swear the big one is the man who attacked us in Wentworth Park. There were four men in the passage at the lock up when I picked them out. Berry never spoke to me when he had seen them. I will take it upon myself to swear that they are the men'.

The witness who had passed the dog cart, Mr Harrison then made his statement. He said that:

'I had occasion to go to Rotherham Bank on the fifth instant and when I got to a place called Cat Lane Pond, which is on the way to Rotherham, I passed two men. After I had passed them five or six yards, one of them said "is this the way to Rotherham". I looked round and noticed them and then answered "yes". After

doing my business at Rotherham, I returned and passed Charles Berry and Robert Myers in a dog cart. In coming through the park, near to a tree which is seated around, I met the same two men again that I had previously passed at the Cat Lane Pond.

I did not speak to them. They passed me one on either side of the grass. That would be about one o'clock. The prisoners I am certain are the men. I noticed them particularly on account of having seen them before. I was first shown the prisoners last Wednesday. They were by themselves. I had previously described them so perfectly that there would be no difficulty in knowing the men. They would be five or six yards from me when they asked if it was the way to Rotherham. One was dressed in a rather darker coloured clothes than the other'.

He described for Mr Whitfield the position of Cat Lane Pond which he said was situated just at the entrance of the park on the road from Rotherham. He stated that Berry and Myers would have been there ten minutes after he had passed. Mr F Falding, the wood agent to Earl Fitzwilliam told the court that:

'I reside at Wentworth. On the forenoon of Saturday the fifth instant while standing in Mr Johnson's butcher's shop at Wentworth, looking out of the window, the two prisoners passed in the direction of Rotherham or Wentworth Park. I spoke to Johnson about them. I have seen the men again and am certain the two prisoners are the men. I have no doubt whatever. These men were shown to me this morning and there was three other men in the passage of the prison when I pointed them out as the men. It was in the middle of the forenoon when they passed Johnson's shop. I noticed them from the manner in which they walked with their heads down and mentioned it to Johnson'

He too stated to Mr Whitfield that he had no doubt they were the same men. Superintendent Green next gave evidence and described arresting Ashton at the Railway Tavern and then continued:

'I took him to the lock up and there placed him in the passage with two other men. I then sent for Charles Berry who identified Ashton as one of the parties concerned in the robbery. The prisoner denied the charge. On Thursday James Darby was brought to me by Sergeant Swinbank one of the Barnsley police, and I charged him with the robbery. On the following day Myers and Berry identified the two prisoners as those concerned in the robbery'.

Mr Hamer told the magistrate that he had twenty witnesses to prove that neither of the two prisoners could have been at Wentworth Park at the time, but Mr Taylor told him it was not necessary to call any more witnesses, after the evidence which they had heard. The two men were found guilty and sent to take their trial at the assizes.

They appeared the Yorkshire Summer Assizes on Friday 12 July 1855 in front of judge Mr Justice Crowder. James Derby and James Ashton were charged with having 'assaulted and robbed Robert Myers of certain money and other property and cutting and wounding Charles Berry at the same time and place'. Mr Blanchard was defence counsel for Ashton and Mr Price defended Derby. Mr Hardy for the prosecution, described the extreme violence used on the two elderly men.

Witnesses were called who gave evidence that Derby and Ashton had been seen in the neighbourhood of Wentworth Park, a very short time before the robbery took place. The defence of both men was that it was a case of mistaken identity. Derby had witnesses called to provide an alibi that he was at Barnsley at the time of the robbery. Ashton also claimed that he was at the Waggon public house in Sheffield when the attack took place. Despite their assertions, the identification of the two men were confirmed by Myers and Berry, and their evidence was corroborated by several other witnesses.

Mr Hardy for the prosecution concluded that the evidence proved that the case against the two prisoners had clearly been made out.

88

The judge summed up the case with 'great minuteness' after which the jury retired, before finding both men guilty, and sentence was deferred. The following day James Ashton, who had a previous conviction, was given six years and James Derby four years imprisonment for the cruel robbery on two elderly men at Wentworth Park.

John Whitaker was an affluent local farmer and cattle dealer who lived at Thrybergh, near Rotherham in 1856. It was said of the elderly farmer that he was worth between £10,000 - £20,000 a year, which was an enormous sum in the nineteenth century. Despite his wealth, it was reputed that he was very careful with his money and he continued to live in a rather dilapidated, small, old fashioned cottage rather than move into somewhere more spacious. Another economy he had was that he would often walk home from the town centre to Thrybergh, rather than go to the expense of hiring a cab.

His friends, knowing his penchant for carrying large amounts of money with him, had advised caution, but he declared that as long as he had his health and strength he would rather walk. On Thursday 16 October Whitaker was returning home from York cattle fair where he had bought 58 sheep for which he paid £120. With £180 still left in his pocket, he reached Masbrough Station at 11.10 pm where, most unusually he decided he would stay in the town for the night.

He went to the Wheatsheaf Inn on Doncastergate where he was well known to the family, only to find that they had gone to bed. Reluctant to disturb them, Whitaker went instead to the nearby Pack Horse Inn on Wellgate, and after enjoying a glass of gin, he changed his mind once again and decided that he would walk home to Thrybergh. Whitaker had reached Dalton Lane End by midnight, when by the light of the moon he saw four men coming towards him, all of them armed with stout sticks and weapons known as life preservers.

The men demanded his money and when Whitaker tried to resist, he was attacked and hit over the head with one of the life preservers. The men then went through his pockets and robbed him of the £180 cash he had brought home from the market. They demanded his watch, but he told them that he had travelled without it that day. The robbers covered Whitaker's face with a cap during the attack, and when they finally left him, he had two overcoats wrapped around his head. Badly injured and covered in blood and dirt, Whitaker managed to crawl to the nearest house owned by a miller named Stringer. He had gone to bed, but his nephew William Widdison answered the door and took in the badly injured man.

On hearing the circumstances Mr Stringer ordered a messenger to be sent to Rotherham to notify the police, and Whitaker was able to tell them that the men had gone in the direction of Dalton Magna. In the meanwhile Whitaker was taken home in a carriage and where the surgeon, Mr Blytheman arrived about 3 am and attended to his injuries. The surgeon found that the injured man had six large scalp wounds, some of which left the bone of the skull exposed. Over the next two days John Whitaker's health slowly deteriorated, and on Saturday morning he died. The local newspaper felt that although Whitaker had left no living relative, that he would be sorely missed by the poor of the parish of Thrybergh to whom he had always been 'a kind hearted friend'.

An inquest was held on Monday 20 October at his own house, where the Coroner told the jury that the proceedings would merely consist of evidence on the identification of the body, until further enquiries could be made by the police. Such evidence was heard, before the inquest was then adjourned to Friday 31 October. When the inquest was reconvened the Chief Constable of Rotherham, Mr Bland told the Coroner that despite several lines of enquiry, no positive identification of the four men had been obtained. He produced a heavy bludgeon still stained with blood, which had been found in a heavily wooded area at Dalton Magna, as well as the life preserver which had been found in a grass field next to the road leading to Rotherham.

He told the court that he thought the robbers had tried to evade the houses at Dalton Brook and had crossed the fields to the Rotherham Road, before proceeding back into the town. The deceased man had made a statement about the attack, but as it was

91

not made in front of a magistrate the statement could not be used as evidence. After hearing from the Chief Constable, the jury returned a verdict of 'wilful murder against some persons unknown'. A reward of £150 had been offered, which was increased to £200 by friends of the deceased man. Despite Mr Whitaker's statement no information was given to the police that lead to the conviction of any of the men.

That should have been the end of the matter.

Twenty six years later in May 1882 a woman called Ellen Leedham made a complaint of ill treatment from her husband to the Sheffield police. The couple were both aged 42 and had lived in the city for some years. Ellen told the police that the previous June her husband Aaron, had confessed that together with his father and another man, named William Siddall they had killed John Whitaker in 1856. Ellen said that she had previously lived on the Wicker in Sheffield and had taken in lodgers, one of whom was Aaron Leedham, who she married in April 1880.

She told them that on one occasion she asked Aaron to accompany her to her sister's house at Dalton Brook, Rotherham and noted how he started at her mention of the place name. He shuddered as he told her 'I think not'. He then asked his wife if she had heard of John Whitaker and she told him that she only knew that he had been murdered many years ago. Aaron admitted the crime, although he said he had only been 16 years of age at the time. As he told her this he began to cry, because he had promised his father on his deathbed that he would never reveal the truth about the attack to anyone.

Whether it was remorse for the crime, or regret that he had told Ellen about it, from that moment on Leedham began to ill treat his wife. In her statement to the police she said that at the same time he began to drink more heavily, and he complained that he 'could not sleep quietly at night'. His cruelty towards her had got so bad that the following July she had been forced to take a warrant out against him, and he had been bound over to keep the peace towards her. Since that time they had lived apart, although the workhouse officials had made her an allowance of 8s a week to keep herself and her two children.

On this money, together with a small cleaning job Ellen managed to eke out a living for herself. Referring to the latest attack on her by her husband she stated that on Sunday 7 May 1882, her husband had gone to the cottage she shared with her children. He had knocked her to the floor and had accused her of having another man in the house. When she protested, he knelt on her breaking three of her ribs. He told her that 'he would make her die a more cruel death than Whitaker, and then he would then hang himself'.

Continuing with her statement she said that after the robbery from Whitaker, Aaron Leedham's father had taken a watch to a jeweller's in London and had the name 'John Whitaker' beaten out of it. This was puzzling as, according to the story given by John Whitaker, he had told the robbers that he didn't have his watch on him on the night of the robbery. Also the Rotherham police had found no mention of a stolen watch in any of his depositions which had been taken at the time. However Ellen said that when the elder Mr Leedham died a few years later, he left the watch to his daughter. The Rotherham police managed to take possession of the supposedly stolen watch, but none of the friends of the deceased man could swear to it being the one owned by John Whitaker.

Aaron Leedham appeared before the Sheffield magistrates on Friday 13 May charged with the assault on his wife. Some hours later he was discharged and given bail. The following day after some enquiries had been made by the Rotherham police, Aaron was re-arrested by Superintendent Hammond and charged with the murder of John Whitaker. He was brought to Rotherham on the 9 pm train where, despite his wife's description of his agitation, he appeared to be very unconcerned about his position.

93

The next day William Siddall of Attercliffe was found and he too was arrested and brought to Rotherham. Aaron had told the Rotherham police that twenty six years previously, the men had been involved in planning the robbery for quite a few weeks before it was carried out. They knew that Mr Whitaker was in the habit of carrying quite a bit of money on his person, and so they carefully watched the road that Whitaker usually travelled on his way home. Despite their vigilance the elderly farmer had always managed to escape them until the night of the robbery.

The two men were brought into the Rotherham Police Court on Monday 15 May 1882 where they were both remanded, until further police enquiries could be made. By the time Aaron was taken into the magistrate's court at Rotherham a few weeks later, he was now claiming that the other three men had actually committed the murder, and he had simply kept watch. Perhaps inevitably after such a long time since the robbery, on Monday 12 June both men were set at liberty, due to lack of evidence against them. Before he could leave the dock however, Aaron was re-arrested on the charge of assaulting his wife. He was brought before the Sheffield Quarter Sessions on Friday 30 June and given a sentence of five months in Wakefield prison.

The question remains as to whether Aaron Leedham had got away with a murder which he had committed 26 years previously. Whilst Ellen Leedham's statement could be taken as retaliatory for the behaviour meted out by her husband, nevertheless if her statement is to be believed, it still lay uncomfortably on the man's conscience many years later.

Chapter Fourteen: The Tragic Death of Thomas Beaumont.

In the days of the nineteenth century the majority of crimes brought before the magistrates were caused by drunkenness. Several Temperance movements had been established in the town to reduce the menace of alcohol to the working man. Petitions were sent to Parliament by such societies, calling for the reduction of public house openings. They also petitioned for them to be closed all together on the Sabbath instead of the partial closing it had at that time. But it had no effect and the incidents of drunkenness continued. Cases were regularly brought before the magistrates and not a few ended in murder. The case of Thomas Beaumont however remains an enigma, was he killed by violence or was it simply an accident?

At 11 pm on Saturday 9 January 1859 three drunken men named Thomas Crowther, Thomas Beaumont and Henry Wilson were making their way home from Rotherham to Kimberworth. Crowther and Wilson knew that their companion was very intoxicated, but concerned about his safety they passed their own houses to see him safely home to his cottage at Kimberworth. As they were wending their way home, Beaumont saw another man enter the house of a 37 year old man called Isaac Westwood, who worked as a furnace worker at the Midland Iron Works. Suddenly Beaumont started to giggle and went towards the door of the cottage.

The two companions watched amused as the drunken man shouted out for Westwood to bring him a half a penny worth of small beer. Westwood came to the door enraged at the noise that the men were making and told them to go away, but Beaumont continued to demand some beer. Westwood came to the door in his shirt and trousers and told Beaumont 'damn you, I'll give you some beer; come here and let's see what you are like' and he chased after the men. Hearing Westwood angry footsteps, the two men, Wilson and Crowther started to run and Beaumont followed behind them.

Westwood, now in a complete rage, pursued Beaumont and catching up to him a violent altercation followed. Beaumont said that he was sorry for annoying Westwood, but this didn't satisfy his attacker. As Beaumont turned to go, it was alleged that Westwood struck him so hard at the back of his neck, that it knocked him over a small wall at the side of the road. Unfortunately at the other side of the wall was a drop of five feet, over which Thomas plunged, landing on a pile of stones at the bottom. The fall so badly injured his spine that he was left completely helpless and unable to move. Westwood then ran after the other two men vowing vengeance on them also.

A little later a man called Arthur Brailsford, who had been working at the Midland Iron Works. was walking along the same road when he heard a cry. He looked over the wall and saw the injured man lying on the stones. He tried to lift him, but it was a difficult task as Beaumont was unable to stand. Thankfully Brailsford heard someone coming and shouted to them to help. It just so happened that it was Isaac Westwood who, unable to catch up with the other two men, was now walking back to his house. Westwood still angry, refused to help as did another man called Abraham James saying that the injured man was just drunk and to leave him.

Somehow Brailsford managed to get Beaumont to the Midland Iron Works, where he sought some assistance. Police Constable Cockcroft was sent for, and when he saw Beaumont, he too assumed that he was drunk. The police officer refused to send for a surgeon or a cab knowing that if he did either and the man was proved to be simply drunk, then he would be forced to pay for it out of his own pocket. Finally, as the man's condition deteriorated to the point where even Cockcroft noted that he was really ill, reluctantly he ordered a cab to take Beaumont to his own home at Kimberworth.

96

Surgeon Mr Crowther was called in to attend to the injured man and he found that the nerves of sensation and movement had entirely gone, and Beaumont was by then insensible. There was little he could do for him except to make him as comfortable as possible. Westwood was arrested and Beaumont died a week later on the following Saturday morning. From a post mortem examination it appeared that death had resulted from a dislocation between the third and fourth vertebrae of the neck. Thankfully two days before he died, Thomas Beaumont had made a dying deposition outlining the events before the Hon. and Rev. W. Howard, solicitor Mr Whitfield and in the presence of the prisoner.

When giving his deposition, Beaumont stated to the effect that he was knocked over a wall separating the road from some fields. He did not see the person who knocked him over, but that he remained there groaning in agony for some time. An inquest was held by Coroner Mr T Badger at the Old Public House, Kimberworth the same evening. Mr Gillett the Superintendent of Police stated that the wall in which the man had been knocked over, was only nine inches high at the side of the road. At the other side however it was a 4 feet 9 inches drop.

The Superintendent told the inquest that when Westwood was charged with assaulting Thomas Beaumont and knocking him over the wall, he had replied 'no, he fell over it'. Arthur Brailsford said that the prisoner worked with him at the Midland Iron Works and that he was a steady character and a good worker. He told the inquest that when he saw the deceased, he thought that he had been sat on the wall and because of his drunken condition had fallen backwards. The Coroner closely questioned PC Cockcroft as to why he had not sent for a surgeon immediately, after finding the man in such a dangerous condition.

The Constable explained that he was frightened that he would have to pay for the cab out of his own pocket. Superintendent Gillett confirmed to the court that in such cases the cost of the surgeon and the cab would not be paid by the parish authorities.

The Coroner stated that this was a terrible state of things and he reprimanded the Constable for failing to get help for the injured man immediately. He told him that if he had done so, it might have saved Beaumont's life.

Solicitor Mr Whitfield called witnesses to prove the good character of the prisoner. One of them was the manager of the Midland Iron Works, Mr William Hartley who agreed with the evidence of Brailsford, and said that Westwood had always been a quiet and inoffensive worker. He told the Coroner that there was a rule at the works which stated that any man who struck another, would be subjected to a fine of 5s. He claimed that the prisoner had never incurred such a fine, although he had been employed there for four years.

Thomas Beaumont's employer, Mr Crowther of Westgate stated that the deceased man had worked as a carter for him for many years. He claimed that Beaumont was usually a steady man and a good worker. After hearing all the evidence the jury found Isaac Westwood guilty of the manslaughter of Thomas Beaumont. They added that:

'we very much regret that a medical man was not sent for Beaumont as soon as he was found, and are of the opinion that the police should have full authority to call in medical aid in all such cases where such aid is required'.

Isaac Westwood was brought before Mr Justice Byles at York Assizes on Tuesday 8 March 1859. The prosecution Mr Maule, described all three of the men as being very drunk and disorderly. He said that the deceased man and his companions had banged on the doors and windows of Mr Westwood's house causing a great commotion at a very late time of night. He also claimed that that the prisoner had been naturally annoyed at persons applying at his house for beer. The defence solicitor Mr Seymour pointed out that the deceased and his companions called at the prisoners house just for a lark and it was not intended to upset Westwood or make him angry.

He said that the prisoners door was partly open and he was sat inside with some companions, thereby inviting someone to knock on the door. He also stated that after Mr Westwood told Beaumont, 'I will give you some small beer damn you, I will', the three men were all laughing as they went peaceably on their way. As far as the three men were concerned the incident was closed. It was only after a few minutes that Westwood decided to follow them and exact his revenge.

The defence counsel stated that it was probable that Beaumont was so intoxicated that he fell over the wall himself as there was simply no evidence to show that the deceased had been knocked over the wall by Westwood. The jury after deliberating the matter returned a verdict of manslaughter, but they strongly recommended the prisoner to mercy on the grounds that they did not think that he had any intention of seriously injuring the deceased. The judge agreed and he simply ordered that Isaac Westwood be imprisoned for just a week.

Chapter Fifteen: The Mangle Woman of Masbrough.

Masbrough suffered from much poverty in nineteenth century Rotherham, and there was little help available for any widow who lost their husband. The only alternatives for those women were to find some kind of employment, or to enter the workhouse. So when Elizabeth Roebuck was left to bring up her four children in 1863, she bought herself a mangle. Now she could not only take in washing, but other poor women, unable to afford such a luxury themselves, would pay her to use it.

Elizabeth was known to be a respectable and hard working woman by the people of the neighbourhood, so she soon attracted the attention of a widower, a plate layer on the Midland Railway. His name was Joseph Thompson and at some point around Christmas of 1863 the couple started a relationship. By the following March, Elizabeth admitted to friends that several times Thompson had asked her to marry him. However soon she heard rumours about his bad temper, and the way he had ill treated his late wife, while she had still been alive. In September of the following year Elizabeth told him that she wanted no more to do with him.

On Thursday 15 September 1864 around 9 pm Thompson left his lodgings on Westgate and went to Elizabeth's house near Windmill Square, Masbrough. He intended to ask her to relent and to take him back. Elizabeth told him categorically that she would never marry him, before asking him to leave her house and not to come back. Women were coming in and out of the house to use the mangle and so he remained there, making small talk until all the women had gone. Without speaking, he then attacked Elizabeth violently, hitting her over the head again and again with a poker he took from the fireplace.

The poor woman grabbed a chair and put it over herself to protect her head, but he smashed the chair and continued with his attack.

Her screams had attracted some of the neighbours, who got hold of Thompson and pulled him away from her. Despite her terrible injuries, he offered his captors money 'to let him have another go at her' and expressed a hope that 'he could finish her off'. Medical aid was sought from Mr Bernard Walker, who found that Elizabeth's skull was fractured, she was covered in blood, and had multiple defensive bruises on her arms. Mr Walker knew that her wounds were very serious and that his patient was in imminent danger of death.

Thompson had run away before any of the neighbours could stop him, but he was quickly caught at the Queens Hotel on Masbrough Street and was arrested. Sergeant Kershaw of the Rotherham police force took him into custody, and charged him with the attempted murder of Elizabeth Roebuck. The Sergeant had been to the victim's house and seen the great deal of blood around the kitchen floor and the chair. He had also found a bloodstained cap belonging to Mrs Roebuck which had been knocked to the floor in the attack.

On Monday 26 September Joseph Thompson was brought before magistrates, Mr F J S Foljambe, J Yates and T Tillotson at the Court house in Rotherham, charged with attempted murder. The medical officer Mr Walker gave evidence that Elizabeth was still too ill to attend, and the prisoner was simply remanded for a week. By the time the court was reconvened again on Monday 3 October Elizabeth was finally well enough to be present. However she was in a very weak state and was allowed a chair to sit in whilst she gave her statement.

By now Thompson had now lost all his former belligerence, and it was reported that he looked pale and nervous. He had not been in the dock long before he appeared to faint away and was carried out of the court by two Constables. A few moments later the prisoner seemed to have recovered, and he too was allowed to sit. Throughout the enquiry he looked beseechingly at Elizabeth, but she kept her eyes firmly on the magistrates and the witness box.

101

She was the first to give her evidence and told the court how the prisoner had visited her house earlier on Thursday 15 September. Elizabeth had informed him that he was not allowed to call on her any more. Thompson told her that he would do as he liked, and she told him that if he did, she would fasten the door against him. Thompson then left for a short while, but despite Elizabeth's first warning he still went back to her house again at 9 pm. Once again he pleaded with her to take him back, promising that he would change if she would only take pity on him. It was difficult for Elizabeth, as other women were coming to the house to use her mangle, and she tried to placate him until they had all left the house.

Finally after the last woman left, he offered her some pork pie he had brought for supper. She refused and he told her that 'it would probably be the last supper they should have together'. She then described to the magistrates the violent attack and how she had pleaded with Thompson to spare her life, but he continued to hit her with the poker. Since the attack she had been in bed for ten days, and that she 'had not been able to do anything since'. The poker was produced in court and it was noted that it was bent through the ferocity of the attack.

Two of her children, her daughter Fanny aged 15 and son Edward aged 13 also gave evidence that Thompson had attacked their mother on the night in question. Edward told the court that to defend his mother he had picked up a long brush and had attempted to hit the man with it, but he had missed him. Mr Walker the surgeon, stated that he had been called to Mrs Roebuck's house on the night of the 15th and found her surrounded by woman applying cold water cloths to her head. Mr Walker stated that her head, face and shoulders were all covered in blood. He said that:

'On examining her head I found on it three contused lacerated wounds, and her skull was fractured in one place. She was also very much bruised about her arms and hands. One of the wounds on her head was 3½ inches in length and the skull was exposed.

102

The other wounds were about 1½ inches in length and half an inch in depth. Her head in several places was very much battered. There was a fear of immediate death from haemorrhage and for six days I considered her life to be in danger. She has not yet fully recovered. A heavy angular instrument, such as the poker produced, would cause the wounds described if used with some force'.

Finally the last prosecution witness was a man called William Allot who was passing the house when he heard cries of 'murder'. When Thompson managed to evade his captors, Allot had followed him back to the Queens Hotel and had held onto him whilst a Police Constable was called. Thompson's defence solicitor Mr Whitfield, told the court that there was no doubt that a very serious offence had been committed. But he claimed that although his client had been charged with attempted murder, when he left the house, Elizabeth was still standing. He pointed out that if the prisoner had truly meant to murder her, he would not stop until he achieved that end.

Mr Whitfield claimed that therefore the charge should have been reduced to one of 'wounding with intent to do grievous bodily harm', which he said appeared to have been borne out by the evidence. His words had no effect on the jury and Joseph Thompson was committed to take his trial at the next Leeds assizes. He was brought into the court at the Yorkshire Assizes on Friday December 16 1864, before Mr Justice Keating. On this occasion the prosecution was Mr Waddy and the prisoner was undefended. Mr Waddy outlined the case for the jury indicating that after the attack the prisoner had showed no remorse.

He stated that on two separate occasions after the prisoner had been arrested and was walking to the Town Hall, he had asked how Mrs Roebuck was. On being told that she was 'still very ill' on both occasions he said 'Thank God, I am a happier man now'. Thompson had conceived the idea that the reason Elizabeth wanted to end the relationship, because she was seeing another man and that therefore the motive had been one of jealousy. Mr

Waddy also pointed out that during the frenzied attack, the prisoner was so intent on killing her, that he had not said a word to her. The jury found him guilty and his Lordship in passing sentence told them:

'A more ferocious attack than that which the prisoner made on Mrs Roebuck, without a shadow of provocation, I never remember to have met with....Looking to the weapon used, the violence and deliberation with which it was used...I would not be discharging my duty if I did not pass upon him a most severe sentence'.

He then sentenced Joseph Thompson to penal servitude for the term of fifteen years.

No doubt the long prison sentence gave Joseph time to reflect on his actions which seemed to be of a calculated and determined nature. The valiant way in which Elizabeth defended herself during the attack, leaving her with massive injuries, indicate a very determined woman. It is to be hoped that she continued with her mangle business in Masbrough and continued to care for her family for many years to come.

Chapter Sixteen: Emma Cutler

At some point around June of 1863 Mrs Waterhouse, a farmers wife of Kilnhurst employed a 22 year old young woman called Emma Cutler as a domestic servant. The girl admitted shortly after she began working for Mr and Mrs Waterhouse that her husband had left her. Soon afterwards however Mrs Waterhouse began to suspect the girl was pregnant, but when she accused her of it, Emma became very resentful and claimed that she was in fact ill and suffering from dropsy. Mrs Waterhouse said no more, but wondered as the girl seemed to get bigger. Eventually in March the girl's condition could no longer be denied and she was given notice and arranged to work her notice.

On Saturday 19 March 1864 the girl disappeared and could not be found. The farmer and his wife searched her room and found unmistakable evidence that she had given birth. The police were informed and on Wednesday 23 March the girl was found at her parents house at Worksop by Police Sergeant Horne and charged with the murder of the child. In answer to the charge that she had caused the death, she said that she had been delivered of a child, but it had been born dead. She then asked Sergeant Horne if he wanted to know where the child was, and when he answered in the affirmative, she told him it was in the attic of Mr and Mrs Whitehouse's farmhouse where she had previously worked.

The body of a newly born female was discovered at the farm as indicated by the prisoner and it was removed to the police office in order to await for an inquest, which was held the following day. The deputy Coroner, Mr W Woodhead opened the inquest at the Rotherham Court House and he told the jury that it would only be a preliminary enquiry. Sergeant Horne of the Rawmarsh Constabulary gave evidence of going to a cottage at Gateford near Worksop on 23 March where the prisoner told him that she had been employed under her maiden name of Emma Neil.

She told him that her married name was Emma Cutler and she was charged with concealment of birth under that name. Emma said that she had buried the child in the attic above the Waterhouse son's bedroom at Kilnhurst and that the child had been born dead. The prisoner cried as she admitted to carrying it into the attic and leaving it there. The Sergeant told the inquest that he then went to the farm of Mr Waterhouse with Police Constable Malesbury and they searched the attic and there they found the body of the child. At this point the deputy Coroner felt that it would be unwise to proceed any further before a post mortem could be made and the inquest was adjourned for a week.

At the re-convened inquest on the afternoon of Thursday 31 March 1864, Emma, who was described as being 'a young woman of very prepossessing appearance' was very distressed, and sobbed throughout the hearing of the evidence. Her mother and sisters were also in the room and the whole scene was described as being very distressing for the whole family. The inquest was told that she had been married for several years, but had not lived with her husband for two years or more.

The house surgeon at the Rotherham Dispensary Mr Henry Darwin gave the jury his findings on the post mortem and he said that had examined the girl on 23 March and found that she had recently given birth to a child. Emma informed him quite voluntarily that she had been in service at the Waterhouse's when she was taken in great pain and had given birth whilst sat at the side of her bed. She had claimed that the child had been born dead and had not made any cry or movement of any kind. Emma told him that she had been unable to react as the baby fell upon the floor.

Mr Darwin examined the child and found no signs of violence externally. It was a full grown female child, rather pale in appearance on the surface of the skin. Internally he found that the lungs were crepliant, showing that there had been respiration, but not to the extent that he could say that the child had lived for any period of time. Therefore he concluded that the child had died from lack of proper medical attention and exposure to cold. The deputy Coroner summed up for the jury and stated that the evidence was quite clear on the mothers own confession that she had been guilty of concealing the birth. The jury without any deliberation returned the recommended verdict in accordance with his instructions.

Emma Cutler was brought before the judge, Mr Justice Keating at the West Riding Assizes on Saturday 13 August 1864 where she was undefended and once again showed signs of great distress during the hearing. Prosecution Mr Vernon Blackburn outlined the case for the jury. Sergeant Horne gave his evidence stating that Emma admitted placing the infant in the attic and again he repeated how she said that the child had been born dead. However, giving evidence herself, Emma told the judge that she had prepared for the birth of the baby to be born at her parents house at Worksop

She had intended going to her parents house after she had served her notice for Mrs Waterhouse and had bought some baby clothes in preparation for the birth. However before she was able to complete her arrangements, the baby came early. However her former employer Mrs Waterhouse told the court that the girl had stayed longer than required after her notice had expired. She was found guilty and as the judge was addressing the jury, Emma fainted and had to be revived.

Continuing, the judge said that the case was entirely devoid of aggravation and he passed a sentence that Emma was to serve just one months imprisonment. Emma Cutler was lucky as previous cases had a death penalty imposed on women convicted of infanticide. Throughout the whole enquiry there was no mention of the man who had got her pregnant, who had taken no responsibility for the girls condition, leaving her in a situation to fend for herself.

Chapter Seventeen: Murderous Assault in All Nations Yard.

One of the most notorious places in Rotherham during the Victorian era was Westgate, as it was a place of slum dwellings, pubs and low lodging houses. The police were regularly called to Westgate to remove drunks, assist in domestic abuse cases and investigate the many crimes that went on in the area. The Rotherham magistrates were tired of hearing cases of crimes which took place on a regular basis along Westgate. As one magistrate commented 'the place was becoming a perfect nuisance'. On the night of Sunday 19 March 1865 a most brutal attack took place, which even shocked those officers attending the scene.

A vicious assault had been made on a woman in one of the alleys off Westgate which was named All Nations Yard. A man named George Hartley, aged 35 lived in one of the small houses there, who was better known in the neighbourhood from his peculiar occupation as 'Muck Jack'. Hartley was employed as a scavenger and was employed at removing night soil [the contents of the toilets] during the dark hours. The man was described by his neighbours as being of the most brutal disposition, who regularly fell out with people around him. Night after night the neighbours were woken and alarmed by the cries and entreaties of his wife, whom he regularly subjected to a beating. Hartley also had arguments with his neighbours and the police were regular visitors to the yard.

Despite the squalor of their surroundings, he and his wife took in lodgers, and it had been noted that in the early part of the previous week, that a labourer called Smith and his wife had gone to lodge in the house. Mrs Ann Smith was the sister of a former wife of Hartley's and it was known that the pair were clearly antagonistic towards each other. That Sunday, Hartley, Mr Smith and their respective wives had been drinking heavily, and as the day went on it was a surprise to no one when they began to get

108

quarrelsome. In the course of the evening neighbours reported yet another noisy dispute taking place.

It seems that Mrs Smith had made some remark, which highly exasperated Hartley and he immediately took her by the shoulders and pushed her out into the yard, shutting the door behind her. She made an attempt to re-enter the house, but as she was opening the door Mrs Smith heard him say 'if she doesn't know when she is well, I will teach her'. Knowing the violent disposition of the man, and fearing the consequences if she persisted in returning back into the house, Mrs Smith changed her mind and she closed the door and walked away.

She had scarcely gone a dozen yards however before Hartley opened the door again. Mrs Smith turned, and in the act of turning Hartley threw with great precision, a large fire poker straight at her. The poker struck her across the temple, and the poor woman, after staggering a few yards, fell heavily against a wall. Neighbours could see blood flowed from her head in streams, as they rushed out to help the injured woman. Hartley, when he saw what he had done, simply went back into his house and closed the door,

Someone called for a doctor, but there were concerns that she would bleed to death before medical assistance could be found. Thankfully Dr Hardwicke's assistant, Dr Edwin Borough was soon in attendance, and on examining the woman he found that the main artery of the temple had been completely severed. He sent her immediately to the hospital, but later that night it was reported that 'she was lying in a most precarious condition and is not expected to live'. Hartley was arrested and taken to the police office.

The news of the murderous attack quickly spread throughout the town and for hours Westgate was thronged with people anxious to visit All Nations Yard to see for themselves where the assault had occurred. It was also reported that:

109

'almost every Saturday and Sunday night during the past winter disgraceful disturbances have taken place in this street. The assault last night is the culmination of a series that have recently taken place'.

George Hartley was brought into the Rotherham Police Court on Monday 20 March 1865 before the Hon. and Rev. Mr Howard and other magistrates. The prisoner was charged with 'cutting and wounding Mrs Ann Smith with intent to do grievous bodily harm'. The facts of the matter were laid before the bench and a remand was asked for, as at that time Mrs Smith was not in any condition to give evidence against him.

When Hartley asked if he had anything to say as to why he had committed the offence, he told the magistrates that the woman came to his house regularly every Sunday in a state of complete drunkenness. Hartley said that when he turned her out the day before, she had struck him in the face and had consequently thrown stones at his door. Without the testimony of Mrs Smith the bench had no option but to remand the prisoner for a week. Hartley was remanded several times in fact, until Monday 10 April when the poor woman was at last in a position to give her version of events. Still visibly suffering from the violent attack of that night, she was brought to the court in a cab.

During her examination she was allowed to remain seated as she made her statement. Mrs Smith appeared to be still excessively weak and her head was still bandaged up, but her condition did not apparently have any effect on the prisoner. He seemed from the minute he entered into the court room, to treat the whole affair with the utmost indifference. The court was silent as Mrs Smith gave her evidence. She told the bench:

'I am the wife of labourer Thomas Smith of Rotherham, and we have been lodging with the prisoner. On Sunday night the 19 March, my husband and I were having a few words about my son, when the prisoner threatened me saying "if I did not hold my tongue, he would put me out of the house". I told him he would

110

not. He jumped up from his chair and opened the door and then turned round to my husband and said 'now lad are you going to turn her out'. 'My husband replied "No I shall not turn her out".

The prisoner then took me by the shoulders and pushed me out into the yard, and shut the door. There was a stone near and I picked it up and threw it at the door, I tried to open it to get back inside but I could not. I then asked him to give me my bonnet and I would go. I called out to him "you are badly George". He answered "If I am not badly, I'll make you badly very soon" I heard him cross the floor as I walked down the yard. When I had gone about a dozen paces, I turned my head around and as I was doing so, I felt something strike me on the head. The prisoner was then standing at the doorstep.

I walked another two or three steps and then fell against a wall, bleeding profusely from the head. I was confined to my bed for three weeks and have not been out the house until this morning. Directly after the blow I looked to the ground and saw a poker'.

A fitter called Arthur Wilson told the court that on that Sunday he had been standing at the back door of the house, where he lived in All Nations Yard. Suddenly he heard raised voices, and he saw Mrs Smith come out of the house of the prisoner and directly afterwards someone shut the door. Mrs Smith tried to push open the door again, but she could not open it. Wilson saw her swear at someone still inside the house, before she turned away and walked down the yard.

The witness described how the prisoner had then come to the door with the poker in his hand. He described how Hartley had poised the poker as if to throw it, and seeing what he was about to do Wilson shouted at him to desist. Ignoring the man's warning Hartley threw the poker and it struck Mrs Smith on the left side of her head. Mr Edwin Borough, the assistant to Dr Hardwicke, was the next to give evidence. He told the magistrates that he had been sent to the house on the night of the assault. There he found his patient to be in a very low state, suffering from a wound on her temple which was about three quarters of an inch in length.

111

The wound was not dangerous, but it caused a great loss of blood. Dr Borough stated that he had attended to Mrs Smith since then, and confirmed that she had been confined to bed for three weeks. He was shown the poker, which was described as 'a fearsome weapon' and he confirmed that it could easily have caused the wound. Police Constable Holgate said that after the assault, he had apprehended the prisoner and charged him with the assault on Mrs Smith, Hartley was shown the poker and he had replied 'I did not strike her with it; I heaved it at her, and would do so again if she came to my house in that state'. However he did confirm that it was the same poker that he had thrown at the woman.

The prisoner in his defence said that Mrs Smith was causing a great disturbance and added that 'she brought the punishment on herself'. After hearing all the evidence the chair of the bench, the Hon. and Rev. Mr Howard told the prisoner that they had found him guilty, and decided to send him to take his trial at the assizes. Hartley appeared to be astonished at this, and said that he would rather it was decided by the magistrates. The bench informed him that they had not the power to do that, given that it was such a violent attack and the prisoner was removed.

It was reported that 'he seemed perfectly astonished to be informed that the charge was too serious a nature to be deal with by the magistrates'. On Tuesday 8 August 1865 George Hartley was brought before judge Mr Justice Mellor at the assizes at Leeds. The prosecution was Mr Waddy and he outlined the case for the jury. Once again Mrs Smith gave her version of events, and in cross examination by the prisoner, who was undefended in court, she hotly denied that she was drunk and abusive at the time of the attack.

The prisoner's only defence was repeating his accusation that she was a drunken and abusive woman. He claimed she was someone:

who spent even the parish allowance in drink. I have borne with her until I was compelled to turn her out of the house, and I threw the poker at her in order to frighten, but not with the intention of seriously wounding her'.

The fact that Hartley admitted that he had no intention of injuring her went along way with the jury. They acquitted the prisoner of the felony, and found him guilty of the lesser misdemeanour of unlawful wounding. His Lordship said there was no doubt the prisoner had received great provocation, but not to an extent which would justify the use of such a weapon. Mr Justice Mellor then told Hartley that as he had been in prison for four months already he must undergo a further imprisonment of just six weeks.

Chapter Eighteen: 'Life's too short'.

This is a curious case of an argument between two men, which without the use of a firearm might not have been taken any further. In fact the two men had made up their quarrel and shook hands, but because of the intervention of a police officer, the process had to be taken down the legal path of the day.

Henry Holden and Samuel Geldard were both furnace men employed at the Yorkshire Engine Works Company based at Meadow Hall near Rotherham in November 1869. Three weeks previously Holden aged 38 had been discharged from his position, and Samuel Geldard had taken his place. Since that time, relations between the two men had quite naturally deteriorated. On Monday night 15 November 1869, Geldard was drinking at the Talbot Hotel, Blackburn, when Holden came in and started to call him 'foul names'.

Holden suggested that Geldard had only got his old position by offering to work for less money, and by casting doubts on his [Holden's] ability to fulfil his duties properly. After listening to his former friend for some time, Geldard decided he had enough and left. Two hours later he returned back to the pub and found Holden still there and just as quarrelsome. At 9 pm he got up to leave urging Geldard to go home, adding 'mind how you get home, you wont have to live long'. Eventually Geldard left in the company of a man called Henry Moss, and they noted that it was a bright moonlit night. After walking approximately fifteen yards from the hotel they both saw Holden.

Geldard looked towards him and then saw him slowly lift his right arm, before hearing the sound of a pistol and seeing a flash. Geldard ran up to his former friend in anger and shook him saying 'I have a good mind to dash your brains out against the wall'. Holden appeared to be completely shaken by events, and when Geldard asked him why he had done it, he replied 'I did not mean to harm you, I hope you will forgive me' and the two men shook hands.

Henry Moss took Holden back to the Talbot Hotel where Police Constable Berry was, and handed him over and Holden once again he asked to be forgiven. Geldard told PC Berry that Holden had left his situation three weeks ago and he had taken his place. At first he appeared quite sanguine about it, but latterly had become more aggressive. He stated:

'Holden complained because I had taken his place at the works. But he did say life was too short and it was no use trying to injure one other. Nevertheless I was in fear on leaving the house, but I don't believe he intended to injure me. I am willing to let the whole thing drop'.

PC Berry however thought differently and Holden was arrested and taken into custody. The prisoner told PC Berry that he was sorry for what had happened and that he was very drunk at the time, and again repeated that he didn't mean to do it. He claimed that he had been shooting at small birds earlier in the day with the pistol and that he had not aimed his gun at Geldard, but was only 'discharging the shot before I went home'. However he was searched and in his possession was a flask of powder, a box containing gun caps and two knives.

PC Berry then took him into custody and Henry Holden was brought into the Rotherham police court on Tuesday 16 November charged with the attempted murder of Samuel Geldard at Blackburn the previous evening. PC Berry gave his evidence to the magistrates and said that he had been on duty at Kimberworth, and was walking down Meadow Hall Road about 11.45 pm on Monday night when he met Henry Moss and some other men who told him about the shooting. The Constable told the magistrates that he had witnessed both Holden and Geldard shaking hands before he arrested the prisoner.

Henry Holden's defence counsel Mr Edwards interrupted at this point and told the magistrate that he objected to the Constable stating anything that the prisoner might have admitted to him, as he had done so under the inducement that he should be forgiven. He pointed out that such statements could not be used in evidence against the prisoner, as hearsay. The bench overruled his objections and PC Berry was allowed to continue with his evidence.

Mr Edwards addressed the bench on behalf of the prisoner and he said that this was a very unusual case, in that the victim, Samuel Geldard himself was very reluctant to prosecute the prisoner. He stated that he did not believe that the prisoner intended to shoot the victim or injure him, and urged the bench not to send him to the assizes. He hoped that the bench would give the prisoner the benefit of any doubt that they might have.

The magistrates however pointed out that even though the prisoner was intoxicated, that he had actually fired the gun and they had no option but to send him to take his trial. Mr Edwards then applied for bail which was refused. On Tuesday 7 December 1869 Henry Holden was brought before judge, Mr Justice Lush at Leeds Town Hall, charged with felonious shooting at Samuel Geldard with intent to kill and murder him. There was also a second charge of shooting at Geldard with intent to do grievous bodily harm.

Mr Blackburn appeared for the prosecution and he outlined the case for the jury. He stated that he truly believed that the prisoner had no intention of hurting Geldard and that he agreed to forgive Holden, before he gave him into the custody of the West Riding Constable PC Berry. Holden was defended by Mr Tennant who made the point that at the time of the shooting, there were other men on the road travelling in the same direction as Samuel Geldard. He pointed out that if the prisoner was intent on shooting to kill Geldard, that he could have done it in a place where there were no other witnesses. Mr Tennant also stated that the victim had not been struck by any bullet, and that if the pistol had been charged with shot he should have been struck.

He claimed that there was in fact nothing in the pistol except powder. His lordship told the jury that they had to decide whether or not the pistol was loaded with a bullet, because if it was not, there had been no felony committed. The judge spoke of the prisoners conduct, although wrong was more of bravado than anything else. The jury found that the pistol had not contained a bullet and the prisoner was found not guilty and discharged.

Sadly, as we have seen, rows in public houses became a common occurrences in Rotherham and all too often these would end up in a death of one of the participants. In the 1870's such a crime took place with regularity in the town to the point that the local newspaper stated that:

'The district of Rotherham seems to be of late prolific in fatal public house quarrels. During this last week, we have reported two cases of drunken rows from Rotherham which have resulted fatally, and now we have now to chronicle a third'.

On 22 September 1873, a man called Henry Hutchinson aged 24 kissed his wife Ann farewell and left their house at Mount Pleasant, Wath to go to work at the Manvers Main colliery. Little did he suspect that before nightfall, he would be involved in a duel that would end his life. Hutchinson completed his days work before calling in at the Gate Inn at Swinton about 4 pm for a drink, before going home for his tea. Several of his work colleagues were there.

A carpenter called William Firth saw Hutchinson and another man, who was a quarryman named William Naylor aged 22, having a drink and both appeared to be sober. Suddenly and without any warning, Firth saw Hutchinson starting to take off his coat and challenge Naylor to a fight. The quarryman told him not to be so stupid, and that he had no intention of fighting anyone. Nevertheless Hutchinson demanded that he come outside and fight a duel and reluctantly Naylor, who was the smaller of the two men, went out of the pub and took off his coat.

Two other men called William Botwood and William Oldfield agreed to acted as 'seconds' and soon a crowd had gathered round. A witness named John Emery saw the men preparing to fight and tried to make them stop, but Hutchinson told him to 'get out of the way'. Someone told Emery that the men were fighting over 'an old grievance, and it was better to get it over and done with'. By now quite a crowd had gathered around the two men, and they watched as the men fought for about two rounds. Despite being the smaller man, Naylor appeared to be winning, and eventually the fight was stopped.

Hutchinson was chaffed about the fact that the smaller man had beaten him by his work colleagues, and suddenly he demanded that they fight again. It was reported that this time the two men 'went into it like two game cocks'. Naylor hit Hutchinson in the mouth and he went down hard, the back of his head hitting the ground violently. He lay still and the men noted that blood was coming out of his mouth. Mr Edward Dibb a surgeon of Mexborough was called in about 4.15 pm, and found that Hutchinson had been carried into a nearby field, adjacent to the Gate Inn. The surgeon noted that his patient was already insensible and he died about twenty minutes later

An inquest was held at the Kings Head Inn, Swinton on Wednesday 24 September in front of Coroner Mr Dossey Wightman Esq., who told the inquest that a man called William Naylor was already in custody charged with causing the man's death. The room was crowded by a large group of men who all worked at the Manvers Main colliery and who had known the dead man. The first to give evidence was Hutchinson's wife, Ann who said that she had last seen her husband alive on the morning of the 22 September when he was going to work. He was then in good health, but the next she saw him he was lying dead at the Gate Inn at Swinton.

William Firth of Swinton, a carpenter said that he was in the Gate Inn when the incident took place. It was about four o'clock and apart from the deceased, there were one or two other men. He described the fight and Hutchinson's death, and added that some bystanders took away the body to the field. He had heard the dead man say as he was going out side to fight with Naylor that 'he could leather a lane full of men such as him'. John Emery of Cliff Field, Swinton, also a collier, stated that no one was present at the

119

commencement of the row except himself. He was walking up the road when Hutchinson came out of the Gate followed by Naylor.

The deceased already had his coat off and Naylor was pulling his coat off and readying himself for the fight. The two men started to fight and Emery described how, at one time it seemed like the two men had locked their legs together, when Hutchinson fell down. Emery told Hutchinson he had better stop as he could see the man Naylor was 'fresh'. Hutchinson complied and he was taking the man inside the Gate when some of his friends came out. They made comments to him about Naylor being smaller than him, but nevertheless had roundly beaten him, when Hutchinson suddenly appeared to change his mind. He declared that he would have another round or two.

The bystanders cheered and they encouraged the two men to carry on with the fight. Emery described for the inquest how the two men started fighting again before they had a short rest. At the time Naylor was sitting near the man named William Botworth, who was acting as his 'second' and the deceased was standing with a man named Michael Oldfield who appeared to be holding him up. After their short rest they started fighting again and suddenly Hutchinson fell to the ground where he then lay still, and the witness saw that he was badly injured. Emery ran to get him some water, but when he came out of the pub with the water, the man was still lying on the ground and Naylor was crying.

He thought that at the commencement of the fight that Naylor seemed drunk, but that Hutchinson appeared to be sober. Hutchinson's wife was sent for and she quickly arrived, but her husband was already unconscious. Emery heard Michael Oldfield, the man who had acted as his second telling Mrs Hutchinson that 'he would not have fought any more but for me'. Surgeon Mr Edward Dibb stated that he had completed a post mortem on the following day and gave his opinion that the deceased man had died of apoplexy, which was the bursting of a blood vessel brought on by the fracture in his skull. He told the inquest that from the evidence, he had believed that the fracture had been caused by a fall, not from the blow.

On the side of his head where he received the blow there was swelling. That would have been quite sufficient to have caused the deceased to feel giddy and to reel and fall. Mr Dibb said that in his examination he had noted that the lungs were also in a diseased state and the brain was far from healthy. The Coroner, Mr Wightman then addressed the jury and told them that the case presented great problems for them. He said that although there was no doubt that the death of Hutchinson had been caused by his fall, he had received his injuries at the hands of William Naylor. The Coroner pointed out that Naylor was at that time 'in the commission of an illegal act, that is fighting'. That being so, they could do nothing but send him for trial for manslaughter.

The inquest was stunned at his next words. Mr Wightman stated that if the jury thought that the two men who had acted as seconds, William Botwood and Michael Oldfield were also involved in the fight, that they should be sent for trial as well. The two men were in the room when Mr Wightman announced that they too would have to be sent for trial, and judging by the look on their faces, this was a most unexpected turn of events. After a short deliberation the jury found a verdict of manslaughter against Naylor only. Nevertheless the two men were shortly afterwards arrested, and all three were brought before the magistrates on Saturday 29 September 1873.

The prosecution, Mr Taylor told the court that the men who were acting as seconds had 'made themselves responsible for any serious consequences that might occur' during the fight, and therefore they would have to answer for Hutchinson's death. The prosecutor pointed out that a clear violation of the law had taken place in the case, and he believed that the bench would deem it necessary to commit all three prisoners for trial at the assizes. To the amazement of all three men, they were found guilty and sent for trial. They were all given bail, Naylor himself for £40 and two sureties of £20 each. The other two prisoners were bailed for £20 each and two sureties of £10.

The following year the three Swinton men, William Naylor aged 22, William Oldfield 35 and William Botwood aged 33 appeared at the Leeds assizes on Saturday 4 April 1874. It was usual that convicted men would usually appear at the assizes within a few months of conviction at the magistrates court, but the legal complexity of this case had led to a delay in bring the case before the Grand Jury. Mr Vernon Blackburn was prosecution and the men all had separate defence counsels, Mr Tennant appeared for Naylor, Mr Lawrence for Oldfield and Mr Waddy QC for Botwood.

The men were tried in a subsidiary court room, before Mr Price QC. Mr Blackburn outlined the case and told the court that the case rested on whether Naylor gave Hutchinson such a blow that had killed him outright, or whether the deceased had died falling backwards onto his head. Mr Blackburn pointed out that the surgeon Mr Dibb was of the opinion that death was due to apoplexy, resulting from a blow or a fall. Another witness had said that such a blow was administered by Naylor, and that blow was the cause of the fall.

Mr Blackburn pointed out that the fact remained that Hutchinson was the more powerful man of the two men, he was the main aggressor, and therefore it could be suggested that Naylor was merely acting in self defence. As to the connection of the other two witnesses in the affair, Mr Blackburn agreed that after the second round, William Oldfield had acted as second for Hutchinson by holding him up. William Botwood had also supported Naylor under the arms after the second round, but there was no other evidence against him. Mr Tennant stated that his client, Naylor right from the start had been unwilling to fight, but that Hutchinson who was a much bigger man had compelled him to do so.

122

In the defence of Botwood, Mr Waddy agreed that the only case that could be made out against him, was that he picked up Hutchinson after he had fallen on the floor. Mr Lawrence defended his client equally well. There was much discussion on the legal complexity of the case which resulted in a consultation between judge Baron Pollock and Mr Price QC. It was finally agreed that as the evidence stood, the case did not come within the range of self defence.

Therefore under the circumstances the prisoners could not be excused from the consequences of their actions. The three men appeared to significantly feel the seriousness of the crime with which they were charged. Thankfully the Grand Jury saw it slightly differently from the more senior legal colleagues and they gave all three men the benefit of the doubt. When they returned back into court they returned a verdict of not guilty and all three men were discharged.

Chapter Twenty: The Swindles of William & Eliza Fritz.

When the tradesmen of Rotherham heard that William Edward Fritz had inherited £4,000 from his wife's uncle, and that he should receive the money on 4 April 1871, they were only too willing to let him have goods on account. He also claimed that he had a large 80 acre farm left to him by his grandmother, and they were really impressed. William even dressed the part and so when he entered the shop of Mr Albert Bibbs, a jeweller of Church Street, Rotherham on 15 March, Mr Bibbs had no reason to doubt his story.

His later statement to the police which was repeated in court described the swindle. He said:

'I am a jeweller and silversmith. The prisoner called at my shop on 15 March last. He told me his wife had £4000 left to her by her uncle and that he should receive it on the 4 April. He also told me that he had a farm left to him by his grandmother, bringing him about £180 a year. He said it was something like 80 acres of land, and it was situated somewhere in the region of Wellingborough, Northamptonshire, I think at a place called Rushton. He talked about coming into possession of it and having £180 coming in at once. I believed him.

He mentioned the name of Mr Worthington of Manchester, and said he was his solicitor, and he was coming down on Monday to arrange with him to go to London to receive this £4,000. Believing those statements I supplied him on 15 March with a lady's gold lever watch, a silver lever watch with a centre seconds, a lady's gold guard chain, a gold Albert chain, a gold locket which was chased and enamelled, and a gold swivel seal amounting in value to about £28 or £29.

On the following day, he and his wife visited my shop. They selected more goods, a gold fringe brooch, a pair of gold fringe

124

earrings and a chased gold keeper ring amounting to £8.0s.6d. He came again on 17 March and had a gold seal and keyring and on the 18 March Mrs Fritz had a pair of spectacles and a case. None of these articles were paid for'.

In order to re-assure the anxious tradesmen Mr and Mrs Fritz invited them to an evening party at his house on 17 March where Mrs Fritz entertained them, by her rendering of a popular song called 'Susan's Sunday Out' which she sang with great enthusiasm. This particular song was about a servant maid who on her day off [or day out] she would bring back stolen items from her employers. The tradesmen of Rotherham should have taken note!

The next day William and Eliza Fritz absconded along with four big boxes and a carpet bag. It was later reported that they took the Leeds train from Rotherham station. Arriving in Leeds they employed a porter of the Midland Railway Company to transport them to Asquith Street, giving the name of Smith. When they arrived at the lodging house of Mrs Ann Doughty of Asquith Street, Leeds, William told her that they were only staying overnight, and that they were going to America the following day.

The next day they left, but instead of going to America they took all their luggage to another house in Cambridge Street, Leeds. It was there that Eliza Fritz was found at 2 pm by Inspector William Horne of Rotherham police on 22 March, armed with a warrant for her and her husband's arrest. The couple were brought back to Rotherham, by train the next day. William and Eliza Fritz were brought before the magistrates on Wednesday 5 April 1871 and the court was packed in every part, mostly from swindled local tradesmen.

It was reported in a local newspaper that 'Rotherham yesterday worked itself into a state of great excitement on the occasion of the examination of William Edward Fritz and his wife, whose exploits will not soon be forgotten, by such tradesmen as were induced to accept their patronage'.

125

Such was the couples notoriety that the song 'Susan's Sunday Out' could be heard all over the town, and it was also reported that a brass band played the tune as they marched through the town. Large crowds of people followed the musicians singing the chorus with great energy, making the town centre ring with their shouts of laughter.

The Court House where the prisoners were due to be examined was densely crowded long before the proceedings were due to start. When the magistrates G W Chambers Esq., H Jubb Esq., and H Otter Esq., took their places, every available inch of space was occupied. What the people of Rotherham were treated to that day, was less of a judicial enquiry and more of a Music Hall routine.

When he was asked to stand, William Fritz surveyed the crowd with a cool and calm indifference. Eliza claimed that she was suffering from a chronic heart complaint and was allowed to sit.

A letter was read out in court from a solicitor from Wakefield, Mr Barrett who was supposed to defend the prisoners, but he refused to come unless he was paid in advance. This news seemed to take away some of the composure of the male prisoner, and so a local solicitor, Mr Edwards attended in his place. Mr Whitfield opened the case at great length giving the details of the case for the bench. The theft from Mr Bibbs was the first charge against William Fritz for obtaining goods by false pretences. The second was a charge of obtaining 100lbs of meat and other articles from Henry Bingham of the Shambles on 12 January 1871.

The butcher told the court

'I let to the prisoner a cottage house in Wellgate in October last. He said he was a joiner working at Messrs Askew's, and so I trusted him with between £1 and £2 up to Christmas. He paid that. About the beginning of January he asked me to trust him for some meat, as he had some property coming to him on the 4 April. He said there was £4,000 left to his wife and it was coming

126

from the East India Company through Mr Worthington of Manchester, solicitor.

I trusted him with about £5 of meat after that. I would not have trusted him if he had not told me about the money. The money he said would be paid in London and Mr Worthington would be there, and his [Fritz's] brother from Spain and all the family would be there too. I was invited to be there. They said the 4 April would be a great day for them, and they would be glad if I would go to London with them'.

There was loud laughter at this comment, before the court was hushed again and his statement continued:

'I went on supplying them with meat until 18 March. I supplied them with meat and bacon to the amount of £9. At the latter end of January, the prisoner said that he had a grandmother at Rushden near Wellingborough in Northamptonshire, and he had received a letter saying that she was dead. He said she had left him a farm and a homestead of about 80 acres and he expected he should have to go over to inter her. He wanted me to lend him £5 and I called and left him that amount at his house in Wellgate the same day.

A short time afterwards I saw him again. He said that he was very glad to inform me that his grandma had behaved so well to him in leaving him that nice estate. He was going to take possession of it on 25 March. I received an invitation to go with him and take possession of it. I saw him again a few days previous to the 18 March. I saw the postman give him some letters. He showed me one and said "this is from my solicitor at Manchester reminding me of the day and the hour". On Saturday morning the 18 March he called in at my shop where he only stayed a few moments.

After hearing the statements about the money I supplied meat to both the prisoner and his wife. On the 18 March I received a note from Mrs Fritz, asking me to get her two and a half couples of fowls, some cauliflowers, a cucumber and a quarter of lamb. I
127

procured all the articles for her but the lamb which I supplied myself. On the Sunday morning following I saw their house on Cemetery Lane, to which they had removed from Wellgate, in the beginning of March. It was then closed and it was closed on the following day, and has been closed ever since'.

He was cross examined by Mr Edwards and was asked about various amounts of money that he had lent the couple. He spoke about being invited to the house one evening with three or four other tradesmen and their wives, where he spent a very pleasant evening. Then a man called Charles Willesden of Brown's Yard, Sheffield gave his evidence. He said:

'I have known the prisoner since last July. We became acquainted by his coming to lodge with me in July last. He and his wife stayed a fortnight. That was the only time he lodged with me, but he has paid many a visit since. The prisoner and his wife were at my house on the 17 January last. Fritz told me that he had been to Northamptonshire to bury his grandmother, who had left him a farm and £500 to stock it after the lease was up, which had about three years to run. She had also left £100 to his wife and £100 to each of his children.

The prisoners stayed at my house until the following evening, and I accompanied them to the Victoria Station and saw them off by the 9.30 pm train from Sheffield to Rotherham. He asked me before he left to buy him a couple of nice rabbits. He wanted the best there was in the market. He took the rabbits with him. Both Mr and Mrs Fritz were both dressed in deep mourning'.

Mr John Worthington, a solicitor practising at Cheadle near Manchester told the court that he had been in practice in the area for about 45 years, and to his knowledge there was no other person who was a solicitor with the same name. He stated categorically that he had no knowledge whatsoever of the prisoner. Another man called Mr George Frederick Packwood told the court he lived at Rushden which was five miles from

Wellingborough in Northamptonshire. He had lived there all his life, which was 54 years.

He was a relieving officer and registrar of births and deaths for the county. He confirmed there was no death lately at Rushden of any lady leaving property. No person named Fritz had died and left a farm, and he also confirmed that he never saw the prisoner to his knowledge. A Rotherham woman, Mrs Mary Warwick of Wellgate then gave her evidence. She said:

'I know Fritz and his wife and have known them about nine months. I remember the 17 January. They told me before this that they had a lot of money left them and on 17 January Mr Fritz told me that he had got a letter from his grandma in Northamptonshire, who was very ill. He told me afterwards that his grandma was dead and they had the blinds drawn'.

Once more there was laughter in the court as the witnessed described the traditional respectful Victorian habit of closing the curtains when a near relative had died.

'They also got some mourning clothes to wear. They went away, and said they were going to grandma's funeral, and they asked me to take charge of the house. They returned the next evening. They had a couple of rabbits with them and Fritz said he had brought them off his grandma's farm, and they had been killed about an hour before he started'.

Mr Edwards intervened at this point and stated that there was simply no evidence in this case on which to commit the prisoners. He said that the butcher Mr Bingham could not swear to lending the prisoner £4, as to whether it was before he had been told about the fortune that was due to them, or afterwards. Therefore the prisoner could not be charged with obtaining credit by false pretences on that particular charge. With respect to the £5 which he said that he had left it at the prisoners house, there was no evidence to show that Mr Fritz or his wife had actually received it, which again could not be charged as having received it by false pretences. Despite Mr Edwards eloquent defence, the bench found William Fritz guilty and the prisoner was then committed to take his trial.

The next charge was then brought against Eliza Fritz by John Law, a draper of Bridgegate. This charge was for 'obtaining 9½ yards of merino and other articles by false pretences at Rotherham on 12 December 1870'. Mr Law told the court:

'I know Mrs Warwick, who has been a regular customer of mine. On the 12 December she came to my shop and said that a Mrs Fritz who lived near her, wanted to receive a few goods on credit until she received some money. I let her have goods to the amount of £7.3s.5d. On 23 January Mrs Fritz said that her husband had lost his grandma and that they required suitable mourning clothes, not to appear beneath the relatives they were about to meet in London on 4 April. The goods were supplied by me on that day amounted to £22.3s.7d.

Mrs Fritz said that she was going to the funeral. After the funeral on 27 January Mrs Fritz came to me again and purchased goods to the amount of £3 odd, and said that grandma had been very kind and considerate to them. She had left a farm of 180 acres, and four legacies of £100 each, one for herself, one for her husband and one each for the two children. On Feb 11 she got £11 worth of goods, including a sable victorine [a woman's fur shawl] and a muff.

Shortly after this I became uneasy from information I had received about 20 February, and I went to Mrs Fritz's house. I saw her and told her that my confidence in her was shaken, and I should like to know from her whether her intentions were honest or not'

Once again there was a shout of laughter in the courtroom when Mr Law uttered those words, but he turned to his fellow tradesmen and told them 'you may laugh gentlemen, but I am quite able to bear your smiles. My back is broad enough to bear it' to which there was renewed laughter. He then continued with his testimony:

'Mrs Fritz said I must speak to her in a gentle manner as she was afflicted with a heart disease. She produced a letter from her solicitor which said that the money to be received from her uncle would be realised, and payable in London on the 4 April. With reference to the goods on 23 January, Mrs Fritz referred me to Mr Bingham, and from the satisfactory reply I received from him, I trusted her'.

Mrs Warwick was re-called and confirmed that she had introduced Mrs Fritz to Mr Law and gave the same story about the expected inheritance. Other similar evidence was given on behalf of Eliza Fritz from various drapers of the town. In total the couple had obtained goods to the amount of £200.

Inspector Horne next gave evidence and said:

'I am Inspector of Police for this district. I went to Leeds in search of the prisoner on 22 March. After making search and enquiry, I got to a cottage house in Cambridge Street. I found the female prisoner in the house. The male prisoner was not in. I waited till he came to the house. I was there from shortly after two o'clock until five or six o'clock.

The male prisoner passed the door, and I sent a police officer out after him. He brought Fritz into the house. As soon as he entered the door I produced a warrant and read it to him. He said "you will find all of the things here: I am sorry its done" I told him I had list from several tradesmen, Mr Bibbs and others with a list of jewellery. He then said "come up stairs". He opened a collar box and I found all the articles produced, the property of Mr Law at the house in which I apprehended Fritz.
The prisoner assisted me to pack the things in boxes'. Mrs Fritz said "we have done it together and I hope we shall suffer together". I took the male prisoner into custody and locked him up in Leeds until the following day, when I brought him to

Rotherham. While he was in custody at Rotherham Mr Gillett asked him if there was anywhere he wished him to write to. Fritz said "No. I shouldn't like to disgrace my friends".

He then proceeded to give similar evidence as the other witnesses, before stating:

'I went to Northamptonshire last Monday. I was in the company of many officers of police. I made diligent enquiries after a lady who had died there lately leaving property, but could hear of nothing of the kind'.

Mr George Hammerton a cab proprietor of Masbrough then told the bench:

'On 18 March last about a quarter past nine in the evening, the prisoner hired a cab from me. He asked if I could fetch some luggage from a house in Cemetery Lane, so as to catch the 9.50 train to Leeds. He went up to Cemetery Lane with me in the cab. He placed in the cab four big boxes, a small one, a carpet bag, a bonnet box and a cured ham. He got inside the cab by himself. I was too late to catch the train. I delivered him and his luggage at the Masbrough Station'.

Daniel Wilson a servant of the Midland Railway Company at Leeds, gave evidence that he had been on duty at the luggage and cloak room when the prisoner deposited his luggage. He gave his name as Smith and he was given a ticket for his luggage. Benjamin Copley a cabman of Leeds stated that he was at the cab stand near the Old Church in Leeds about noon on 19 March. The prisoner asked him to get some luggage from the Midland Station.

He gave the cabman the luggage ticket in the name of Smith whilst he remained outside. The boxes were taken to Asquith Street, Leeds. At this point in the case a brass band struck up outside the Court House, and several people shouted out 'Susan's Sunday Out'. There was much hilarity in the court and even the prisoner indulged in a smile. Ann Doughty, a widow of Asquith

Street, Leeds gave evidence that the prisoner and his wife had arrived at her house about 1.30 pm on 19 March. Fritz told her that he had got the promise of some work.

At this point once again the brass band passed the court again 'playing with even greater spirit'. Several individuals in the gallery attempted to sing a chorus of 'Susan's Sunday Out', but the police were quick at silencing them. The examination continued and Mrs Doughty stated that the couple only stayed on the Sunday night, and on the Monday Mrs Fritz said that they were going to the post office to look for a letter, and then they were going to America. They took their luggage away about two o'clock.

Another witness was Robert Walker Eastwood of Leeds who stated that the prisoner applied for a house giving his name as Fritson Smith. The prisoners were found guilty on this charge before the third charge was dealt with. This was for obtaining goods to the amount of £62 by false pretences from Mr Aaron Phillips, a draper of College Street, Rotherham. He stated that Fritz had visited his shop on 3 March and told a similar tale to him, stating that he was about inherit £4,000 from a relative in India, and was about to claim his estate at Rushden. He continued:

'he had invited Mr Haggard and Mr Bingham to go with him go with him to receive this estate. I congratulated him heartily. On 14 March the prisoner and his wife came to my shop. I told them I was exceedingly glad to see them [to which, again there was much laughter in court]. He told me they wanted a few articles to furnish their house for when Mr Worthington from Manchester came to see them on 20 March. They selected a nice assortment of curtain, rugs etc. to furnish a house to the amount of £9.9s.1½d.

At the same time they selected patterns of carpets and gave the orders for them. I got the carpets made at once. They came to about £8. Fritz came again on 6 March, stating that he was afraid that the carpets would not be done by the time Mr Worthington

133

came. The lawyer was coming to make out Mrs Fritz's will, as she suffered from heart disease, and it would be a serious matter if she died and the will was not made out. I supplied goods to the amount of £15.14s.8d. He afterwards came to be measured for two suits of clothes.

One was for every day wear and the other was to be the very best I could produce. He wanted them to go to London to receive the money. I supplied the suits to him. He ordered his wife a black silk velvet mantle. I got it made for her, and the price was £10. The last interview I had with her was on 10 March when she said she was disappointed that the mantle was not ready. I am very glad it was not as I did not see her again. On Monday the mantle arrived and I sent it to her house, which was shut up. Altogether I supplied £52 worth of goods excluding the mantle'.

There was a sensation in the court when he revealed the amount of money which he was owed. He was followed by three pawnbrokers of Leeds, who had also advanced money on items sold to them by the prisoner, who had given several false names. The prosecution, Mr Whitfield told the court that there were five other charges outstanding, but he did not think it necessary to go into them at present.

Fritz defence solicitor Mr Edwards pointed out that the majority of the goods had been recovered from the Fritz who had handed them over quite readily. He asked for bail but at that point Superintendent Gillett brought forward a letter he had received from Glasgow. It was dated April 4 1871 and although it was badly written, it obliterated any feelings of sympathy that the court, and particularly the misguided tradesmen, might have had for the couple.

The unsigned letter was read out and it seems that Mrs Fritz, who had called herself Mrs Edward Wright, was as much to blame in swindling tradesmen as her 'husband'. It said:

'Sir, I received yours on the third and the description you gave of Edward Wright, for I believe it is the proper name of his wife. I have no doubt she was never married to him and she is the greatest swindler of the two. She received money off my wife and never paid for the goods, besides money and a tin travelling trunk. I have had to pay £1.2s and also £3.12s for groceries unknown to us in our name. [here he listed several people to whom they owed a total of £57.6s] He took a partner in a joiners shop in one of the principal streets of the city, got £5 of his partner and left him with the shop on his hands, and a great number of smaller accounts from £1 upwards too numerous to mention'.

The letter writer then went on to state that Mrs Fritz had obtained the goods and that she had expectation of £1,800 which she was due to draw on 25 July last. Instead the couple had left Glasgow on 23 July to allegedly go to London to pick up the inheritance, and they were due to return on 27 July to pay off all her debts. The unnamed letter writer stated that he had given the Superintendent's letter to the Glasgow police. He concluded:

'so you see he has done it pretty well in Glasgow. In your description of her saying she squints, she is blind of one eye, but it is not closed. If you can get any of our good back for us, we shall be very thankful if we have a little to pay for them. Please to send me a newspaper with all the perticulars in, or any other expense that you may occur and I will remit it you by return of post'.

The letter concluded the whole of the evidence against the two prisoners and they both pleaded not guilty. When William was asked if he wanted to speak in his defence, he stated that 'he was sorry but there were many things in law he didn't understand'. When Eliza was asked if she wanted to say anything, her husband spoke for her. He claimed that she had committed the offences whilst under his direction, and therefore she was not guilty. The jury returned a verdict of guilty for both, and the chair said to

135

them that they would both be imprisoned and kept to hard labour for 15 calendar months.

In a postscript to this case it seems that Mrs Fritz, although a clever deceiver of gullible people who were prepared to extend goods and money on account, had been telling the truth about her health. News on 8 June 1871 reached Rotherham of the death of Mrs Eliza Fritz aged 45 at the Wakefield House of Correction. When admitted to the gaol she had complained of pains in her chest, and was therefore employed in the more gentle task of sewing at the prison.

It seems that during her term of imprisonment, Mrs Fritz had several stays in the prison hospital, before dying of a heart condition just two months later. The verdict given was 'death from natural causes'. There is little doubt that not many tears would have been spilled from Rotherham's tradesmen, duped by this notorious couple during their stay here.

Chapter Twenty One: Eliza Uttley.

As we have already seen there were many cases of young unmarried girls finding themselves pregnant in Rotherham and having to deal with the consequences. In this next case, even though the girl implicated a respectable young doctor of Masbrough, her dying confession could not be heard because of a legal technicality.

In the year of 1871 Eliza Uttley was aged 26 and was a domestic servant working for Mrs Sharpe of Moorgate Close, Rotherham, when she found herself in a most difficult position. At some time around the 6 September she found that she was pregnant and she claimed that the putative father, was a 32 year old surgeon's assistant, Mr William Collinson of Masbrough. According to a later deposition that she made, Eliza said that she had been four months pregnant and when she confronted him with the fact, he told her 'he would get shut of the child'.

In the same deposition she saw that he used an instrument on her, which she described as being 'silver and long'. After the operation Eliza went back to the house where she was employed about 10pm, and went straight to bed. She tried to get up to go to work the next day, but was unable to, and as a consequence she was dismissed on Friday 9 September. Eliza called a cab which took her to her mother's house at Greasbrough to recuperate.

On Sunday 11 September she was so ill that her mother sent for Collinson to attend her. When he examined her in her bedroom, he asked her if she had 'got rid of it' and she told him 'yes'. The girl remained ill until a qualified physician, Dr John Charles Hall was called in to see her the next day. He quickly realised that she was suffering from peritonitis, and would probably not recover and the girl was rushed to the Rotherham Hospital. Dr Hall warned her that her life was in great danger, and when she asked him if he thought she would get better, he admitted that she would not.

She then described the above circumstances and it was agreed that she would make a formal dying deposition. She was attended by hospital surgeon Dr Long who asked that Mr Jubb, the magistrate was to be sent for and Mr John Oxley the clerk to the magistrates, to write down the deposition. Eliza then made the statement which was read out to her and she signed it, as did Mr Jubb. Sadly Eliza Uttley died at 4.30 am on Wednesday 14 September 1871.

Collinson was brought into the Rotherham Police court later that day, charged with 'having used certain instruments with intent to procure an abortion on a certain woman named Eliza Uttley'. William Collinson was well known in the town and as a consequence the case had created quite stir. The local newspaper commented:

'A very painful rumour has been current in Rotherham for the last day or two, relative to a gentleman who has for a long time past, occupied a respectable position in Masbrough. Very grave and serious charges were laid against him, and a confirmation of the report appeared to be given on Wednesday morning, by the apprehension of the gentleman in question'.

Mr Edwards appeared for the prosecution and it was reported that he told the court that 'it was with the greatest regret that he had undertaken the prosecution of Mr Collinson, who he hoped after this enquiry would be able to clear himself and leave the court without a stain on his character'. However when he proceeded to give evidence as to the death of Eliza Uttley, Mr Edwards stated that:

'he would show that her death had been caused by the use of an instrument by the prisoner to procure an abortion. The declaration made by the girl would prove that she was pregnant by the prisoner, and when she went and told him of the circumstances, he proposed and she assented, that instruments would be used to get rid of the child.

138

This had resulted in her being prematurely delivered of a child which had died and it had resulted in her own death. As an inquest was about to be held on the woman's body, and the results of the post mortem heard, he should after that be prepared to go more fully into the case than he would do so at that moment'.

Her father Sampson Uttley gave evidence that his daughter had died in the early hours of the morning at Westfield House, Red Hill, Greasbrough where he lived. Dr Long the hospital surgeon stated that:

'I attended the deceased on Monday night last at nine o'clock. I examined her and found that she was suffering from peritonitis or inflammation of the membranes of the cavity of the abdomen. I cannot give any explanation as to the cause of that. It would be impossible to give any other reason than supposition. I examined the woman only casually, because she was in very great pain and I considered it was not right to put her to a great deal of trouble in her examination.

I saw her the next morning and examined her, and from what I saw I concluded that she had a miscarriage and that peritonitis had resulted from that. I have seen the foetus this morning. I have not examined it minutely, but I should say it was about five months advanced'.

He was cross-examined by Mr Whitfield, and he told him that peritonitis could arise from a variety of causes. In a manner which betrayed the ignorance of many surgeons of his time, he claimed that if a woman had a normal pregnancy and caught a cold that could cause her to develop peritonitis. It might also occur in cases of anything affecting the bowels. Henry Jubb Esq., Justice of the Peace stated that he had taken the statement from the deceased and produced it in court.

He declared that both Dr Long and Mr Oxley had been present when the deposition was taken, but that Collinson was not there when the girl made the statement. Mr Edwards said that there

139

were grave objections to the deposition being read out in court, and claimed that it was not admissible as evidence. This was because the girl had not been put under oath at the time she had made the statement, to which the magistrates agreed. Mr Edwards then applied to have the prisoner remanded and Mr Whitfield stated that he had no objection. The prisoner was then remanded until the following Monday.

The inquest was held later that day at the home where the deceased girl had died, at Westfield House, Greasbrough, before Coroner Mr John Webster Esq. The prisoner was not in attendance, as he was still in the police cells at Rotherham, but Mr Whitfield appeared to watch the proceedings on his behalf. Mr H J Knight was the first to give evidence, and he explained that he had held the post mortem that morning. He stated that the girl had been pregnant and had died from peritonitis.

When asked if he could give a reason for the death, he stated clearly that it was from an abortion. Two other doctors who had been with him at the post mortem, Dr Hall and his assistant Mr Charles Moore agreed with his findings. He was asked several technical questions on the reason for the peritonitis, which he answered to the best of his ability. When he was asked if a man would have to have specialist knowledge to procure an abortion, he answered in the negative. Inspector Howe had brought a catheter to the inquest, and the doctor was asked if such an instrument could have been used in such an operation, and he agreed that it might.

He was also asked if such an instrument could be used to draw water from the bladder, and he agreed again that it could. Dr John Charles Hall described how the deceased woman had given her deposition and that during it she appeared to be a great pain, pressing her hand to her side frequently. He said that her face was bathed in perspiration, and she sounded and looked completely exhausted. When he was with her on the Sunday at her house, he saw William Collinson coming up the stairs. Dr Hall stated that he met him at the bedroom door.

140

He told the inquest that he had heard that Collinson had been out to patients 'doing a little of what we call quacking'. Dr Hall asked him if he had seen the patient before, and he told him that he had and that he had sent her an aperient mixture [used to move the bowels]. Hall tasted the medicine and it was as Collinson had said. Dr Hall told him that the girl had miscarried and Collinson denied that any medicine he had sent her would do such a thing. After Collinson had left, Dr Hall went to the bedroom and asked Miss Uttley if she had been 'in trouble'. When the Coroner asked him what that meant, he explained that woman who are single and find themselves pregnant say they are 'in trouble'. The girl answered 'don't tell my mother' and also said 'I have got shut of it'.

Dr Hall said that he saw Collinson again after the girl had made her deposition, and he told him that she had accused him of using an instrument to procure an abortion. Collinson denied this and he told him that he had only drawn water from her. Dr Hall told the Coroner that he had attended the post mortem, and saw that there were no signs of injury on the external parts of the body, and assumed that a simple catheter had been used in the operation.

Elizabeth Lockwood of Greasbrough was the next witness, and her evidence showed how the body of the child had been found in the privy at Westfield House. Inspector Horne then stated that on the previous Wednesday morning:

'I took William Collinson into custody on a warrant which I read to him, charging him with causing a miscarriage on a woman named Eliza Uttley by using an instrument. He handed to me the instrument produced [the catheter] and said "that is the instrument I used; but not for that purpose". On Thursday morning, the last witness pointed out to me a certain place. I caused the place to be emptied and found the body of a child, which I gave to Mr Knight.'

The Coroner then stated:

141

'I will not conceal from you the fact that there is a dying declaration made by Eliza Uttley, which is here today, but which cannot be laid before you, chiefly because there is no one who can prove it. It is only right that a dying declaration should be laid before you if the law will allow me to make you acquainted with it.

Therefore I shall adjourn this inquest, in order that we may have the opportunity of looking more fully into the law, and seeing whether I can allow the declaration to be laid before you; and if so, in order that we may have witnesses present to prove that this woman made that declaration. We cannot do anything more today'.

The inquest was then adjourned to Tuesday 19 September 1871 at the Flying Dutchman at Parkgate, when once gain the difficulty about the declaration was introduced. The Coroner stated that although he could not produce the document, he could take evidence of the people who witnessed it. He then called Dr Long who stated that he known William Collinson since March of 1870 and he too was aware that he was practising as a midwife, although he was not sure if he had any qualifications.

He said that the deposition had been taken on 12 September after he told the dying woman that her life was in great danger. He asked her if she had a miscarriage and Eliza replied that she had. She told him:

'I went to Mr Collinson the druggist and he gave me a bottle of medicine. I took only two doses; the rest was thrown away. He made use of an instrument when I was in the room behind his shop. I miscarried. I was between four and five month gone. I was once before in the family way. He used the instrument a week last Wednesday'

142

Dr Long then described the post mortem. Mr John Oxley clerk to the Rotherham magistrates was next examined. He told the Coroner:

'I went with Mr Jubb the magistrate to see this woman and Dr Long went with us. We went for the purpose of taking her dying declaration. She made the declaration but not upon oath. She told me that she thought she was dying and she felt a sinking sensation as if she thought she should die any minute. She told me that she had been to see Collinson and told him she was between three and four months gone in the family way by him.

She said she had a child by him already and I asked who is the father and she replied Collinson is the father of the child. She said she got shut of the child in bed. She concluded with these words." I do not think I shall get better".

Mr Oxley then told the Coroner that Mr Jubb read the deposition out to Eliza and asked her if it was correct, and she said it was. Dr Long also agreed that it was correct. Surgeon, Mr Knight also stated that he knew William Collinson and said that he was the assistant to Mr Edward Robinson, and it was part of his duty to be sent to midwifery cases.

The Coroner at this point stated that he felt it would be useful to have William Collinson attend, and the inquest was adjourned for half an hour whilst he was sent for. When the surgeon's assistant arrived in the company of Inspector Howe, the Coroner asked him if he wanted to make a statement and he said that he did. Collinson said:

'I am a druggist of Rotherham. I am not guilty. It is not true that she was pregnant by me and she never charged me with being the father of the child. When she came to me it would be about 20 August last, she complained of great pain and said that she had not passed water for three days. I used the catheter and took away a pint of water and she was very relieved. She did not tell me that she was pregnant. I saw no more of her until her mother

143

sent for me on Sunday 11 September and I found her very ill. I gave her an aperient mixture and told her that if she got any worse, she was to call a doctor. That is all I have to say'

The Coroner told the jury that the case was not difficult, and that he was very aware that without the girls declaration, there would be nothing to charge the prisoner with. In such cases the law allows them to allow the deposition to be given in evidence if the person feels that he or she is about to die. However the main point that the jury would have to consider is a decision about which version of the evidence they believed. The jury took about half an hour to find William Collinson guilty of manslaughter, and he was given bail with two sureties of £100 each.

Collinson was brought into the magistrates court in Rotherham on Monday 25 September 1871. The court was crowded, as there had been much excitement in the town since the Coroners inquest. Mr Edwards for the prosecution, stated that the law provided that when a man committed a felony, and that felony resulted in death, the crime would be that of murder. This man was charged with procuring an abortion which was a felony and from this act death had resulted.

Mr Whitfield as defence, deprecated the charge of murder being made towards his client, as the Coroner's jury had only recorded a verdict of manslaughter. He concluded that with the evidence that had been heard so far, that no jury in the world would find the prisoner guilty of murder. The bench asked the prisoner if he had anything to say and he told them 'I am entirely innocent'. After a short consultation, the chair of the bench said they felt it to be their duty to commit the prisoner for trial for murder. There was a sensation in the court at these words and on this occasion, bail was refused.

On Thursday 7 December 1871, William Collinson was brought before Mr Baron Pigott at the Leeds Town Hall. After hearing all the evidence, the judge pointed out that the decision the jury had to make was whether the catheter was used for an innocent or

144

guilty purpose. Baron Piggott stated that the doctor had proved that an instrument had been used on the girl, and the prisoner had admitted to using that same instrument for an innocent purpose. He found it difficult to believe that a girl would tell untruths on her deathbed, but he stated that there was no doubt that she was a participator in the offence. He said that:

'the practice had always been to tell juries that where a person was implicated in the guilt, and made a statement against the accused, they ought to look for some confirmation of it before placing implicit reliance on it'.

The judge said they also could not discount Collinson's statement that he was not the father of the child. The jury after a very brief consultation found the surgeon's assistant not guilty and he was discharged.

William Collinson returned to Rotherham and continued in his line of work as chemist and druggist. On 18 April 1874 he was brought before the courts again charged with using light weights, but the magistrates accused him of carelessness rather then fraud, and warned him to be more careful in the future, before fining him just 10s including costs. In June 1879 there was an account of a Mr William Collinson passing his exams in 'the science and practice of medicine' at the Apothecaries Hall in London.

Now fully qualified, in December 1881 Collinson gave evidence at an inquest of an illegitimate child who had died, and in the report he was described as 'a surgeon' and he was still practising at Masbrough. It seems that he was described to be a surgeon specialising in obstetrics in a local newspaper in December 1893. A midwife had been charged with neglect and he had been brought into a confinement case where the mother and child had died. The ignorant midwife was found guilty and sent to take her trial.

There is little doubt that William Collinson went on to have a successful career as a surgeon in Rotherham. When dealing with

145

other pregnant woman, I wonder if he ever spared a thought for Eliza Uttley and how he had come so close to ruin and losing everything?

The crime of abduction was made effective in the nineteenth century as a law to protect women and young girls. Some girls as young as 12 and 13 were found to be working as prostitutes and philanthropists were outraged and determined to rescue children from what they saw as this moral danger. In Rotherham there were two very different cases of abduction, one purporting to be undertaken through 'love' and the other for a much more sinister reason.

It was quite common for very young children to be employed in a variety of positions. Parents found work for them almost as soon as they were old enough for employment, which was often as young as eight or ten years. Boys would often work with their parents in the vast number of workshops and factories of the town, many of them receiving no pay at all. Girls, if they were lucky, might be found work sewing, cleaning, taking in washing or other jobs within the domestic sphere.

One such girl was Emma Allison who was aged 14 and the daughter of William Allison of Hooton Levitt near Maltby. In 1872 she had been employed for the past six months as a nurse to the children of a relative called Mr Wood, a farmer of Ravenfield. It was while she was working there that she made the acquaintance of another young person, 16 year old Alfred Hall who was employed as a farm servant. Despite their very young age the couple fell in love, and on the night of 14 May 1872 they decided to run away together.

They left the home of Mr Wood at some time between 4 am and 5 am, taking with them their spare clothes in a bundle. It was barely light as they walked into the town of Rotherham, before catching a train to Doncaster, where they stayed for a few weeks living as man and wife. When the couple were missed, numerous enquiries were set in place by Emma's distraught family and her friends. Despite their vigilance all their enquiries proved unsuccessful.

Emma's mother finally took out a warrant against Alfred Hall for the abduction of her daughter, but at that time the police were unable to find the couple.

On the morning of Monday 17 June, Emma arrived back at her mothers house at Hooton Levitt. She had gone to the house, not to re-assure her mother of her safety, but simply to pick up some more clothes. The police were called and the girl was detained at the house, where she was closely questioned about Hall's whereabouts. She told the police and her mother that the pair had returned back to live in Rotherham, without the knowledge of anyone who knew them. Despite the local police's diligence, the couple had continued to live as man and wife, under an assumed name at a house near Bow Bridge.

Hall was now working as a miner at the Rotherham Main Colliery. Later that day, about 4.30 pm Inspector Horne of the Rotherham police force apprehended Hall as he was going home from his shift at the coal mine and he was arrested. When he was brought into court the following day, he appeared before magistrate James Yates Esq., charged with the abduction of Emma Allison without the consent of her parents. He pleaded guilty and was remanded for three days until the police made further enquiries.

On Thursday 20 June 1872 Alfred Hall appeared once again in front of magistrate James Yates Esq., and Mr J Otter Esq., at the Rotherham Police Court. Mr Willis was the prosecution and Mr F Parker Rhodes acted for the prisoner. Alfred Hall's mother was at the court and she tried to defend her son for his actions. She told the magistrates that although he was 16 years of age, he was very immature, and that as a consequence was very easily led.

Emma's parents also gave evidence of their concern, when they were told by Mr Wood that their daughter had eloped with his farm servant. They described the search for the pair and their distress at not being able to find their daughter. The next witness was Emma's employer Mr Wood who stated that the girl had been very well behaved whilst she had worked for him, and he truly believed that she had been strongly influenced to run away by Hall. At this point in the proceedings a private conversation took place between the two solicitors, the parents of both parties and the prisoner himself.

Finally the chair of the magistrates Mr Otter addressed Alfred Hall directly. He told him:

'Mrs Allison is disposed to withdraw this charge against you on one condition, and that is that you conduct yourself properly for the future. If ever you show the least disposition to induce, or try to induce this girl to go away with you again, depend upon it you will be severely punished and sent to prison. It will be much the worse for you if ever you attempt such a thing again. Now will you give the promise to do this?'

The prisoner told him that if he were liberated, he would never have anything more to do with Emma again. The prisoner was dismissed and it was reported that he left the court with his mother, who was taking him back to her house at Clifton near Conisborough. Once back home she kept her promise made to the magistrates that she would 'keep an eye' on him. The girl Emma who had not been in the courtroom, promised her parents on their return to Hooton Levitt, never to seek her amorous abductor ever again.

The previous year another little girl had been abducted, but in this case it was much more menacing as she was taken advantage of by a man who lodged with the family. In November 1871, Benjamin Wadsworth aged 24 was staying at the Effingham Arms, Bradgate with landlord Jonas and Mary Roddis and their daughter Anne aged 13. He had been lodging at the Inn for three months and was working at a boiler works at Masbrough, although he had recently become unemployed.

Wadsworth had run short of money and when he asked Mary Roddis for a loan and she refused, he plotted his evil revenge.

149

Anne's mother sent her daughter for some fish around 7 pm on the evening of Tuesday 29 November 1871 and whilst she was on this errand, Anne met Wadsworth in a lane. He made certain proposals to her and induced the girl to go with him, and he kept her with him for the next two nights, wandering about in the area. Thankfully her father met the pair at 4 pm on Thursday 31 November on the road between Barnsley and Sheffield, although Wadsworth quickly ran off. Jonas Roddis took the girl home and the police were called.

When Anne was interviewed she told them that she did not want to go with Wadsworth, but he had used force and violence on her. Anne was asked if she had been unhappy living with her parents and she told the police that hadn't and had 'lived very comfortably at home with her mother and father'. A warrant was taken out for Wadsworth's arrest and he was finally found in Sheffield on 2 December. The following Monday he was brought before the magistrates at the West Riding Court at Rotherham Town Hall, charged with the crime of abduction.

Surgeon Mr William Saville of High Street Rotherham had found no 'marks of violence upon any portion of the girl's person', but he had found 'evidence that indecent liberties had been taken with her'. Wadsworth was found guilty and sent to take his trial at the next Assizes where he appeared before judge Mr Justice Quain on Monday 1 April 1872. His Lordship told the court that:

'This was one of the worst cases of the kind that had ever come under my notice. Because the mother refused to lend him some money, he actually out of spite, took away from her parents this little girl, defiled her in the most shameful manner and for several days dragged her round the countryside until she was rescued. A more atrocious offence than that it was difficult to conceive. I do not understand how it was that he was not charged with rape, then I would have been able to inflict a more adequate punishment.

Turning to the prisoner he told him 'I will give you the utmost the law would allow and that is two years imprisonment'.

Clearly the judges hands were tied because of the man being charged with the lesser charge of abduction and the medical evidence which revealed only that 'indecent liberties' had been taken. Nevertheless the vulnerability of these two young girls is horrific to our modern ears. Incredibly, it is a matter of actual fact that it was not until 1885 that the age of consent in Britain was raised to 16 years.

Chapter Twenty Three: Attempted Murder on the Canal side.

Domestic violence was one of the commonest crimes which was brought before the Rotherham magistrates on a regular basis. During the nineteenth century there was little methods of preventing abuse from happening and little recourse to law for women. As a result the fine line between assault and actual murder was a very close one. Few determined husbands were as determined as the next case and a woman almost lost her life at the side of the canal, if it were not for the intervention of two strangers.

In June of 1873, a twenty two year old collier named George Nixon married his childhood sweetheart Sarah Ann who was aged only 16. The marriage was not a happy one, mainly due to the fact that George was extremely jealous of his young wife, and that as a consequence he acted very violently towards her. After one serious assault at Barnsley, where the couple were then living, Sarah Ann took out a warrant against him, and George was forced to appear before the magistrates.

He was ordered to live peaceably with his wife on sureties for his own good behaviour. George remained unrepentant however, and soon after this attack on 30 November the couple decided to separate. Sarah Ann returned back to Rotherham to live with her parents, whilst he stayed in Barnsley. Within a matter of weeks, George gave up his employment and followed his wife to Rotherham, where he managed to get lodgings on Wellgate. He visited Sarah at her parents house, and after he obtaining employment at Denaby Main Colliery, George convinced her that he was going to 'turn over a new leaf' and Sarah agreed to give the marriage another try.

On Friday 18 December 1873 George persuaded his wife to go for a walk with him that evening, along the canal bank near to the Northfield Iron works. The couple were accompanied by Sarah's

14 year old brother, William Henry. They had arrived at a secluded spot by the bridge at Parkgate when George asked his wife where she had been, and given his jealous nature she made a very curious reply. Sarah told him that 'she had been where she was going again'.

Obviously George understood the reference and he lost his temper and grabbing her by the hair, he threw her on the ground. At this point Sarah had enough and she told him that she would 'fetch him up before the magistrates again'. In reply George stated that 'he would kill her before he allowed her to do that again'. Pulling out his clasp knife he attempted to stab her in the throat. Whether it was due to her struggles, or her young brother trying to pull the man off his sister, George only succeeded in stabbing at her collar bone inflicting little damage.

Determine to still Sarah's struggles, her husband then straddled her body and attempted to stab her again. The desperate girl raised her hands to defend herself, and as a result George slashed her right thumb almost in two. Throwing his knife down in anger, he then attempted to carry her bodily and throw her in the water to drown in the canal. He had almost succeeded when her cries for help attracted two men to the scene, who quickly separated the couple.

Sarah got to her feet and ran into Rotherham still bleeding profusely from her wounds. Arriving at the police station, she gave a statement to Sergeant Turner. The injured woman pointed out her husband who had followed her, and said 'that was the man who attacked me'. Turner promptly arrested George, and when the Sergeant asked him why he had done it his prisoner simply stated that 'he was determined to kill her'. Meanwhile Sarah was being treated by surgeon Mr W H Pearce, who found that although there was plenty of blood, her wounds were superficial.

On Monday 22 December 1873 George was brought to the Rotherham Police Court charged with the attempted murder of his wife. Sarah gave evidence that she left her husband at Barnsley on

153

30 November and returned to Rotherham. On Thursday 10 December George came to Rotherham and asked her to go back to live with him if he got work in Rotherham and she agreed. But then he lost his temper and struck her in the street.

On the Friday 18 December she agreed to meeting him again and described what happened as he tried to kill her. One of the men who had rescued the girl was called John Doherty and he told the magistrates that when the two men heard cries of 'murder' they found the woman laying on her back on the path with her head hanging over the side of the canal. Kneeling over her was the prisoner who had his hands raised as it to hit her.

When he saw Doherty approach he lowered his hand, but he told him 'if you hadn't come I would have murdered her and thrown her into the cut'. Sergeant Turner gave evidence that it was about 6 pm when the woman approached him in College Yard, and pointing out her husband. He promptly arrested him and produced the knife used in the assault. He was asked by the bench if the prisoner had been sober at the time, and Turner stated that he was. George claimed that he had acted out of passion, as he had heard that his wife had deceived him with another man, and repeated again that he would 'do for his wife when he got out of prison'.

The jury consulted only for a short time before finding him guilty. George Nixon was brought before the Leeds Assizes on Monday 6 April 1874 in front of judge, Mr Baron Pollock. The judge told him that 'the attack was a very determined one and if not for the intervention of the two men, he might be facing a more serious charge'. Mr Vernon Blackburn, his defence counsel, told the court that his client had acted under the most provoking circumstances, and emphasised the fact that the wounds inflicted on his wife were only of a superficial nature.

The jury agreed and they returned a verdict that the prisoner was not guilty of attempted murder, but guilty of the lesser charge of wounding with intent to do grievous bodily harm. The judge then sentenced him to 18 months imprisonment.

Chapter Twenty Four: Murder in the Dusty Miller.

On Tuesday 30 October 1876 at 8.50pm, it was a quiet night in the Dusty Miller public house on Westgate, Rotherham. Sitting in the bar were the landlord Mr George Oldfield and his wife, their twenty year old domestic servant Mary Jane Beech and her 25 year old collier husband, James. The fifth person who made up the group was a moulder named William Steer. Mary Jane and her husband had been married in March of that year. James had been a widower who had been left with a small child when he met Mary Jane, and after their marriage, the child was being brought up by its grandmother.

However after only a few months of marriage, the couple had been separated when James Beech was imprisoned in Wakefield Gaol. He had been given four months for the ill treatment of his own parents. James had a history of violence and during their short married life there were several attacks he made on his wife. During his confinement, Mary Jane answered an advert for a domestic servant at the Dusty Miller, where she admitted to the landlord George Oldfield that her husband was serving time.

After completing his sentence, James returned to his wife and they resumed their turbulent married life. At her husbands insistence, Mary had given up her position in the Dusty Miller, and they set up house at Denaby where he began working as a collier. However it was only four weeks later when James again attacked his wife and she left him to return to live at Rotherham. Mary Jane went to see her former employers at the public house and was gladly given back her previous position.

On the morning of Tuesday 31 October, James Beech had shown up at the Dusty Miller and had lounged about for most of the day, begging Mary Jane to come outside with him, saying that he had something to say to her. She told him that he could 'say it just as easily in front of the others'. The landlady, Mrs Oldfield told her not to go outside with him, and they all breathed a sigh of relief when James left the pub at 5 pm. However he was soon back and continued to ask his wife to step outside with him at 6.30 and 7 pm, but doubting his intentions she still refused.

In order to placate the man, the other man in the Dusty Miller that night, William Steer ordered a drink and urged James to join him. To everyone's relief he agreed, and taking off his hat he stated to the company 'here's to fortune and perhaps the last'. He asked Mary Jane for a light for his pipe, but before she could get him a match, William Steer supplied him with one. It was noted that James gave Steer 'a far from friendly glance'.

In the silence that followed, James continued to stare at his former wife to the point where she became suspicious. Noting that he had his hand in his pocket she asked what he had in it, and without saying another word James pulled out a pistol and fired it at her. Steer managed to knock the pistol out of the man's hand, and the landlord George Oldfield, hearing a noise in the kitchen, grabbed him by the neck.

Thankfully it was seen that the cap of the pistol had exploded, but that the charge of powder and shot had not been ignited. James threatened Steer who was still holding onto him 'I'll do you next'. He fumbled in his other pocket, but George Oldfield prevented him from taking out a second pistol. James was held down on the floor, and within a few minutes Police Constable Berry arrived. When arrested for the attempted murder of his wife, the prisoner had told him 'when I fired that shot I intended to kill her'.

When James Beech was in court the next morning, it transpired that he had bought the two pistols for 5s from a shop belonging to gunsmith Mr Needham in the High Street, Rotherham at 5 pm. It would seem that James had made up his mind to kill Mary Jane and left the Dusty Miller to go straight to Mr Needham's shop to buy the guns. After Mr Needham gave his evidence the prisoner was remanded until Thursday 2 November 1876. When he appeared again Police Constable Berry told the magistrates that when he took the prisoner into custody he replied 'I have nowt to say to thee'.

On the way to the police station a crowd gathered as he was walking the prisoner through the streets. Some of the crowd called out that he ought to be hanged and James had said to them 'I wish I had shot the bitch, I would like to swing for her'. He repeated those words again when he was formerly charged. When asked if he would like to give a statement as to why he should not be sent to take his trial at the Assizes, James refused and the Rotherham magistrates had no option but to send him to take his trial at the Leeds Assizes where he appeared on Wednesday 13 December.

James Beech was charged with 'feloniously shooting his wife with intent to murder her'. The prosecution Mr Harold Thomas told the court that the prisoner should be very thankful that he was not facing them charged with the more serious offence of murder. He had examined the case and found grounds of premeditation in that the prisoner had loitered about the Dusty Miller all day in the hope of completing his intentions. He had bought the weapons with the same intention and it was only by being foiled by the other people in the house, that the attempt failed.

Mary Jane Beech gave evidence as her abusive life with the prisoner before his defence counsel, Mr Tindal Atkinson objected to her giving evidence against her husband. The judge disagreed and she was allowed to continue her statement. She described the events of the night and how only the cap exploded before the gun was taken off him by Steer. He also described the attack and how the prisoner told him 'I'll do you Steer' as he held his wrists, before he put him on the floor and disarming him of the second pistol.

Mr Tindal Atkinson told the jury that he did not intend to dispute the facts which had been proved. He told the jury they had to bear in mind that the prisoner 'had loaded the pistol with the wrong kind of powder, and therefore it was a weapon that was as

158

harmless as if it had not been loaded at all'. He said that he had not used a bullet, but mere shot, which suggested to him that he meant to do his wife some grievous harm, but not murder her.

The judge told the court 'he had not the shadow of doubt that the prisoner had gone to the public house prepared with two pistols in the event that one would not go off, so determined was he that his wife would die'. The jury found him guilty and before he was sentenced he asked the prisoner if he had anything to say. Beech replied with deep emotion 'have mercy on me my lord'

Mr Baron Hawkins sternly told him

'it was a merciful intervention of Providence which prevented the pistol from going off and causing the death of your wife. If the pistol had gone off...and as a consequence of it your wife had been killed, you would have stood in the dock to receive the sentence of death and most assuredly you would have died for the crime'

He then sentenced James Beech to penal servitude for 20 years. The prisoner despite his desperate plea for mercy showed no remorse as he was led out of the dock.

Chapter Twenty Five: The Wanton Wife of Kilnhurst.

In yet another case of domestic violence brought before the Rotherham magistrates on Monday 14 July 1879 when a man called Arthur Foster aged 28, was charged with a serious assault on his wife Emma at Kilnhurst. Yet this case would not prove to be as simple as it first seemed, and only when the case was taken before the Assizes, was a completely different conclusion arrived at.

It seems that a month earlier Foster had been apprehended by PC Pilmore for the offence, when he stated that he had found his wife in their outside toilet with another man called Arthur Cookson. He said that being 'thus aggravated' he struck her over the head and demanded that she go back into the house, but she declined and so 'he gave her some more' and she ended up in hospital. The Chief Constable informed the court that since the assault, his wife had developed acute inflammation of the brain, and it was doubtful that she would live.

As a consequence of her poor health, the magistrates agreed that a dying deposition would be taken from her, and Foster was told that as a result of his wife's poorly condition, he would remain in custody. A surgeon, Mr Rowland Hill, told the court that he had examined Mrs Emma Foster and found that she was suffering from extreme nervous disability, with occasional delirium caused by inflammation of the brain She was so debilitated that she was unable to leave her bed or walk without assistance.

That was the situation on the following afternoon when Mr H Otter JP arrived at the hospital to take Mrs Foster's deposition, where he found that the prisoner was not in attendance, but was represented by solicitor Mr G T Barrass. House surgeon Rowland Hill was also in attendance. Mrs Foster totally denied the allegations made against her by her husband and instead gave a long and rambling statement describing her husband's attack.

160

Emma testified that it had started in the kitchen, when she accused him of throwing some flour all over the kitchen floor and table.

She told him that 'if he were a man he would not do that' upon which he swore at her, and said that he would put her out of the house. Emma claimed that he got hold of her by the shoulders and dragged her into the yard, and he grabbed a knife telling her he would 'let her entrails out'. She succeeded in getting away from him, but her husband followed her, and struck her several blows on the head with his fists. He then pulled her down on the ground by her hair and again struck her.

At this point Emma continued with her improbable tale and alleged that she got up and shouted 'murder' before running down the street. Her husband had followed her and that was when a man came up and informed him that 'if he were a man, he would not treat his wife like that'. Nevertheless the prisoner struck her more blows on the head, and she fell on some palisading nearby, saying 'I am a dead woman. Oh do fetch my sister'. Then Emma claimed that another man called George Sellers came up, and she leaned on his shoulders 'until she became sensible again'.

Mr Otter tried to keep her on track as the woman rambled on describing how she was taken to her sister's house and her husband was prevented from following her. Emma Foster told the magistrate and the surgeon that it was not the first time the prisoner had threatened to murder her. About three months ago when she was ill in bed and had the doctor attending her, her husband took hold of her in an attempt to throw her out of the window. She said that he had often stood over her with a knife, and had slept with a razor under his pillow, threatening her that if she slept he would murder her.

As a result she had him at the Rotherham Police Court several times, where he had been bound over to keep the peace. He always promised before the court to behave better, but instead of that became worse. Emma claimed that he had never, since the

161

beginning of their marriage, used her well, and that she dared not live with him if she recovered. She assured the bench that she lived 'in danger of her life' and had to 'go to her mother's on many a night or she would have surely been murdered'.

Emma stated that the prisoner had not supported her, and it was 'only by her mothers aid that she had kept from starvation'. Meanwhile her husband regularly went to Rotherham and spent his money 'in a bad way'. Emma was asked by Mr Otter if the prisoner had said anything to her before the assault had been committed, and she told him that he said nothing except swearing at her. Mrs Foster claimed that there was no reason for the rows, apart from the fact that he did not bring enough money home.

At this point Arthur Foster's solicitor, Mr Barrass tried to establish some truth in what she was saying. He cross-examined her and in reply she told him that whilst her husband was having supper, she did not say that she was going out, nor did she go to the closet [toilet] at that time. The woman claimed that it was much later when she was dragged out of the closet. She said that she had never crossed the yard with a man called Arthur Cookson on the night of the assault, nor did she speak to him that night. Instead she stated that her husband was always 'onto her about men' and if he was to see her speak to one, he would say she was 'thick with him'.

Emma said that the prisoner had not charged her with being with Cookson as a reason for the assault. Mr Barrass asked her if she knew the man who had prevented her husband from striking her, but she said that she did not know him. Continuing with her tale, she then told Mr Otter that on a Saturday three weeks before the assault, she was at her mother's house, and returned home between eight and nine and went out again'. Her replies to the questioning had been so rambling and obtuse that at this point the hospital surgeon Mr Hill stood up and interrupted her digressive testimony. He told Mr Otter that 'his patience could not stand the strain any longer that day' and the deposition meeting was quickly adjourned.

Two days later Arthur Foster was brought into court again before magistrates G W Chambers Esq., H Otter Esq., and C Wright Esq. Mr Parker Rhodes represented the prisoner. A certificate from Mr Hill was put before the bench, which said that Mrs Emma Foster continued to be in a critical condition and was unable to leave her bed. He stated that she was still suffering from extreme prostration from shock to the system, consequent upon an acute attack of inflammation of the brain.

The prisoner was remanded for another week in the hope that his wife would have recovered sufficiently to attend the court. Due to the continuing precarious condition of Mrs Foster however, it was decided that on Monday 25 August 1879 that the case would go ahead. After hearing all the evidence, Arthur Foster was found guilty of the charge of unlawfully wounding his wife on 14 June last, and he was sent to take his trial at the Leeds Assizes.

On Thursday 6 November 1879 Arthur Foster appeared at the Assizes before Mr Justice Bowen, when the motive for the assault was seriously questioned. The prosecution counsel, Mr Lockwood stated that on the night in question the prisoner had gone home, and had some conversation with his wife previous to his taking some supper. She had offended him in some way or other, when he took her by the shoulders and put her out into the yard. Having done that, the prisoner then went into the house and came out with a knife, where he threatened to cut her entrails out.

The prosecution claimed that the evidence did not show that the prisoner hurt his wife with the knife, but it clearly proved that he had some intention of doing her some serious injury. Mr Lockwood told the judge that Mrs Foster was still unable to be present and that her life was still considered to be in very grave danger. Arthur Foster, in his own defence, told the judge the true circumstances of the reason for the argument was when he found her in the toilet with the man Cookson.

163

His first witness for the defence was a young girl of 14 years of age, called Sarah Wilson. She told the court that Mrs Foster had sent her to fetch Arthur Cookson to her house, on at least a dozen previous occasions in her husbands absence. A neighbour called Annie Smith stated that she had seen Ellen Foster and Arthur Cookson going into the back yard, where the toilet was situated quite regularly. She had witnessed the prisoner finding his wife and Cookson together, and had witnessed Cookson running away.

Another witness for the defence was a woman called Ann Farrell. She stated that she had known Arthur Foster for four years, and that she believed him to be a quiet and respectable man, but that his wife was a 'thoroughly bad character'. She stated that even though Mrs Foster had been very poorly after the assault, that 'no neighbour would visit her at the hospital or help her in any way' because of her behaviour to her husband.

A local doctor, Mr Cobb stated that he had attended to Mrs Foster for three months and that she was suffering from a 'bad disorder', which was probably a euphemism for a sexually transmitted disease. The prisoner then addressed the jury and told them that he had frequently heard from other people that his wife was associating with Cookson, but that he hadn't believed it until he saw it for himself. The judge told the jury that:

'if a man found his wife was unfaithful to him, it was no wonder that his blood was heated, no wonder that he did things that a reasonable and sober minded man would not wish to do. If the prisoner had on the spot discovered his wife in her unfaithfulness to him, he might have been so blinded with passion as not to know what he was doing. But how ever much a husband was wronged, if he had time to allow his reason to get the better of his momentary passion, the law knew no excuse for this act of violence'.

He warned the jury that their sympathies might be with the wronged husband, but they had to judge on the evidence alone. The jury returned with a verdict of guilty, but recommended a

164

light sentence because of his great provocation, and the sentencing was deferred to the following day. When Arthur Foster was brought back into court, the judge told him that because of the provocation and the fact that he had already spent two months in prison, he would sentence him to just six more weeks.

Chapter Twenty Six: The Murderous Lodger.

This next case is an intriguing one, full of sexual desire, but whether that passion was returned or not remains to be seen. The letters which were read out in court seemed to have been reciprocated by the woman, initially at least. However the research does not indicate what the husbands feelings were. Did he become a willing cuckold or was it all in the twisted mind of his lodger and former friend? I will let you decide.

In October of 1880 Thomas Doherty was aged 30, and an Irish man who had a wife living in Lancashire. He had been lodging for the last five months with a married couple, William Fleming and his wife Emily who lived at Parkgate, Rotherham. Both Thomas and William were employed at the Parkgate Ironworks where the men had become friends and so when William offered Thomas to become his lodger, his friend readily agreed.

However trouble started as William's wife Emily was very attractive, and it was not long before the lodger was paying her some attention. Eventually Thomas told Emily that despite the existence of his wife in Lancashire, that he had wanted to elope with her, but she had refused his offer and told William about it. William immediately threw the lodger out on 11 September and he hoped that would be the end of the matter. Thomas was not so easily put off however and he continued to bombard Emily with letters.

His letters were a mixture of loving and threatening words as he begged her to come away with him, at the same time threatening that if she did not comply with his request, he would shoot her. In order to evade his threats Emily decided that she would go on an extended visit to some relatives in Stamford where she remained for five weeks, hoping that by the time she returned that Thomas would have calmed down. On her return on 25 September however she found several letters from him, one dated October 16 which read:

'Emily, dearest Emily,
Oh my heart at this moment is overburdened. The burden is too
great for me to carry. Emily you have by your words and acts
brought me to this miserable position, in which I am now placed.
You have brought me to ruin and the destruction of my life. You
have given me cause to commit a dreadful crime, a thing I did not
believe in. You know that I am heartily sorry that I ever saw your
face. Oh is there anything on this earth so dangerous as falseness.

Dearest, you know the pledges and promises which were made
between me and you. I have kept all mine to the letter, but you
have violated every particle of yours. You should not do so. My
heart is overcome with emotion. My tears are flowing fast over
this statement which I write here, But the hard and false heart
which have caused these tears of mine to flow, I am sorry to say, I
will bring to submission. And as I cannot find peace for my heart
any other way, I am determined to face death'.

The letter continues in this vein and begs her to consider which
course she is going to adopt and to let him know her decision by
first post on Monday afternoon. He begs her to write nothing,
unless it is to the effect that she will leave Rotherham with him at
a moments notice, taking only her youngest child with her.
Threatening again to kill himself he concludes:

'I have come to the determination to die for you, so I am ready to
do so. I here swear a firm and solemn oath on this bible I hold in
my hand this moment, that I will sacrifice my life for yours and
that inside of nine days, unless you have me apprehended. I have
given you the best opportunity of doing so, as you can produce
this note against me and then it will my turn next. So you can get
a warrant out for my arrest at once. You know how you have
treated me. Oh I am not the first who died through being deceived
by a false heart.
Signed Thomas Doherty'.

As the threats became more real, William was so concerned about his wife's safety that in her absence he moved from the house where they had been living at Parkgate, to a house in Shaftesbury Square, Eastwood. But it was only later that he found out that Thomas had tracked them down and moved to lodgings in Kenneth Street which were only 50 yards away from the house rented by the Flemings. Now the pursuit of his wife, became much more sinister.

On Tuesday 19 October 1880 Emily was in the town centre walking along Effingham Street near to a shop run by Mr C Laycock chemist and druggist, when she met up with Thomas. He put something that she could not see over her face and told her that he would kill her, but Emily managed to escape and ran into a nearby house. Thomas disappeared and she went home and told her husband about the incident. As she had made arrangements to go out again that afternoon to visit a relative that lived in Old Model Lodging House Yard on Wellgate, William agreed to accompany her.

The couple had just turned into Wellgate at about 3.30 pm when they spotted Thomas, and saw that he had in his hand, a six chambered revolver. He put the gun to William's head, but Emily had the presence of mind to push her husband hard, and they heard the gun go off twice in quick succession. They both ran inside the Cleaver Inn run by Mr Thomas Robinson on Wellgate and Emily held the door to the inn closed. Thomas, however was determined and managed to push the door open wide enough to fire again, and a bullet entered her wrist.

Meanwhile the inhabitants of Wellgate hearing the sounds of shooting rushed out of the houses and shops, and were horrified when they saw the man waving the gun around, and attempting to push open the doors to the Cleaver inn. Thankfully by this time other people from inside the public house were also using pressure to keep the gates to the yard closed. William meanwhile, ran back into the yard of the inn and he picked up a butchers cleaver. He flung it at Thomas with great force, striking him in the left knee and he fell to the ground.

At this point and despite the wound in his leg, when he caught sight of Fleming again Thomas got to his feet and attempted to follow him back inside the Cleaver Inn. He fired once more at him and Inspector Inman who was nearby, heard the shooting. The Inspector, with great courage grasped the gunman around the arms preventing him from firing again. With the assistance of Mr W J Kenning a provision dealer of Wellgate, Thomas was taken to the police station. On the way they were met by Police Sergeant Halliwell who offered his assistance.

On arrival at the station Thomas's knee was examined by the police surgeon, Dr Knight. He found the wound to be a large one which was two inches long and a quarter of an inch deep, which he stitched up. After Thomas had his knee attended to, he was helped into the police cell with the aid of two constables. His knee appeared to be very stiff and he walked with some difficulty. Throughout his capture, Thomas remained calm and cool as he told Inspector Inman that he had fully intended to kill both Mr and Mrs Fleming. When the Inspector examined the gun he found that four bullets had been fired, and two more remained in the barrel.

Meanwhile, back on Wellgate, the police surgeon, Dr Knight had driven up in his horse and carriage. He went inside the Cleaver Inn and seeing Emily in a fainting state and her hand covered in blood he quickly attended to the wound, before taking her to the Rotherham Hospital. There the bullet was removed from her right wrist by house surgeon Dr John Lewis Jacquet and she was allowed to return home. Thomas Doherty was brought before the magistrates on Wednesday 20 October 1880 charged with shooting with intent to murder Emily and William Fleming.

News of the shooting had been widely reported in Rotherham, and a large number of persons had already collected in College Square to see the prisoner. However on the instructions of the magistrates, it was made clear to them that no one would be allowed into the courtroom.

Thomas was brought in between two constables, limping from the injury to his knee where the butchers cleaver had struck it. Despite his injuries he gave the impression of greatest determination and coolness before he was remanded for a week. On Friday 22 October the Mayor, Alderman Marsh told him:

'Now Thomas Doherty you were before me on Wednesday and you were then remanded until today; and in consequence of your present state of health and the state of the woman Fleming, who was also wounded, and for the convenience of both of you. I shall further remand the case until Thursday morning at the Court House at eleven o'clock. Do you understand?'

To which the prisoner replied 'yes sir'. The Mayor then asked Superintendent Hammond how Mrs Fleming was progressing and was told that she was progressing very satisfactorily, and had seen her that very morning walking to the hospital. Thomas then told the Mayor that he would need to communicate with several people he wanted to act as character witnesses for him and he was instructed to give their names to Inspector Hammond. On 26 October Thomas, still anxious to connect with Emily wrote from the Rotherham Town Hall:

Dear Emily,
I write these few lines to you hoping that you will let me know how you are getting on. I have not heard a word about you since my apprehension. I have asked about you many times, but could get no information at all. I hope you will fully consider the state of my mind from Saturday before I committed the act that I am now charged with. I hope that you will write by return or bring a note to the office yourself as you are going by. Please let me know how you are, particularly your hand. Also I wish to know what you are going to do in this case.

170

Please drop me a note early....I think there is no necessity for me to state the cause that drove me to commit the act that I did. It is coming to a nice end now between me and you, but I hope to see you again before I die. I expect you have got all that you wanted now I am out of the way for the present, but I hope not for ever, so I conclude by saying goodbye for the present'.
Thomas Doherty.

On Thursday 28 October 1880 the Court House was filled with people and the gallery was more crowded than other parts of the courtroom. The case was opened by Mr Parker Rhodes for the prosecution. He told the jury that he intended to prove that the attempted murder was premeditated and the prisoner was a determined character who was resolute in taking the action that he did. Emily Fleming gave evidence that on one occasion she was at Sheffield station when she met the prisoner. He conversed with her, and lifting up one of her children placed it in a train nearby telling her that he would buy the tickets.

She assumed that the train was going back to Rotherham but the train ended up in Chesterfield. Thomas realised his mistake and offered to get a bedroom for her. But when he made it plain that he intended to stay the night with her, she refused and as a consequence, they both stayed up all night. He told her that her husband would not believe her when she told him that she had stayed up all night. As a consequence she was apprehensive, however nothing happened. Soon after Thomas told her that he intended to shoot them both and threatened suicide if she did not go to live with him.

At this point in the court Thomas said to her 'Now Emily, I say, You must stop it' and he attempted to climb over the dock rails in order to attack her. Almost immediately two constables entered the dock and restrained the prisoner and the enquiry was resumed. Throughout the examination Thomas called Emily names casting doubt on her memory and calling her 'a nasty woman and a villainous looking creature'. He stated that they were all lying

171

about him, even the court officials and 'that not a single word that the counsel had spoken was true'.

He shouted at her 'can a human heart bear proceedings of this kind' and stated that her own children knew the truth about his dealings with her. At this point with feelings running high, the Mayor adjourned the inquiry in order to give the prisoner time to calm down. Holding hard onto their charge Thomas was bundled away to the police cells.

Three quarters of an hour later Emily continued to give evidence, describing how she had met him on the 19 October on Effingham Street, and how he once again asked her to go away with him. She refused and he told her that he would 'give her something that would do her good' and he pulled out something out of his pocket that 'glittered' but she managed to escape into a house and away from him. The court was silent as she then described the attack on Wellgate. Throughout her testimony the prisoner continued to question her regarding the affair they had.

At one point he asked her 'how many times she had kissed him on the mouth' and 'how many times they had been alone in the house together' but each time she declined to answer. In frustration he told her 'I consider my case very bad, but I consider yours dreadfully worse'. The Mayor told him that even if all the allegations he had made were true, they simply had no bearing on the charges against him. Thomas replied that the counsel for the prosecution had stated that he had forced himself upon Mrs Fleming, when the fact was that she had actually offered herself to him'.

At this point Emily said 'Oh you brute' and she looked relieved as she had finished her testimony.
What William Fleming's thoughts were as he took the stand was unreadable on his face. He too described the shooting on Wellgate and the relationship between himself and his lodger. The counsel for the defence cross-examined him and reluctantly he admitted having a pint of beer with the prisoner at the Grafton Hotel on the
172

morning of the shooting. He reluctantly admitted that Thomas had told him that he had the gun in his pocket at that time.

The defence stated that Thomas could have killed him there and then if he had wanted to, and William was forced to admit that it was possible. Several other witnesses gave evidence to the shooting on Wellgate. Inspector Inman stated that when he had gone to arrest the prisoner, he told him 'I'll not shoot you officer, its those people there I want to shoot' pointing at William and Emily Fleming. When one of the witnesses accused him of shooting the woman through the hand, Thomas had replied 'I should have been better satisfied if I had shot her through her false heart'.

Inspector Inman said that whilst in custody the prisoner had written a letter to Emily Fleming and had asked Inspector Inman to post it for him. The inspector had delivered the letter and also brought back one written from Emily Fleming to the prisoner. At the same time she had handed him a packet of letters that Thomas had written to her. Mr Henry Walford, a pawnbrokers assistant of Effingham Street, Rotherham stated that on the 18 October, Thomas had purchased a six chambered gun from him for 7s, and the following day he was seen around the town looking for Mr and Mrs Fleming.

After hearing all the evidence the jury quickly found Thomas Doherty guilty and asked that he be committed for trial. The prisoner then made a statement, he said:

'I have to state that I never intended - never had any intention whatever of doing William Fleming any harm, never in my life. With regard to the firing of the shot, I cannot swear to it, as I consider that my mind was not in a fit state at the time to know what I was really doing. I had, as I have said, a pint of beer with him on the morning of the occurrence, and if it was my intention to do that man any harm, I have had all the opportunity that a man could require. There was no person whatever or anything or

anything else to hinder, if I had thought fit to shoot the man when we were in the Grafton Hotel'.

On Tuesday 9 November 1880, Thomas Doherty was brought before Mr Justice Field at the Leeds Assizes. The prosecution stated at the outset that he was simply presenting the case of attempted murder of Emily Fleming in order to show the case was 'deliberate, designed, matured and executed' by the prisoner. Emily Fleming produced the letters that he had sent to her and one that had been sent from her to him was read out. The letter said:

'Dear Tom,
I hope you will not do anything rash for my sake. Dear Tom, I shall not go to any public officer for a warrant. I have more respect for you than that. Tom, you ought to think what I have gone through. Write to me an answer and all things will come right'.

She then described the events of the 19 October. When he was given the opportunity to speak, Thomas said that he had bought the gun, but only to frighten Emily into coming to live with him, and in order to do so he had let it be known that he had a gun in his possession. He said that he had lived in the house for four months as her husband, although her husband was still living there. Initially she had returned his affections and had collected his wages for him when he asked her to.

On several occasions she had agreed to live with him 'where ever he wanted to go'. Emily had sent him letters saying as much, but he had burnt them at her request and the change in her manner towards him had 'driven him mad'. In an attempt to gain the sympathy of the jury, he told them that he had suffered much pain from the wound in the leg made by the cleaver. The jury were unmoved as they found him guilty and the judge stated that he had 'never had a more wicked or unprovoked attempt at murder before him'. He told the prisoner that he:

'was a married man living in a house with another married man and his wife, and trying to persuade that woman to leave her husband. You had given the woman your wages that you might indulge your lust with the wife of another man, though you have a wife in Lancashire. The woman said - and I believe her - that she had resisted you. You bought a revolver and loaded six chambers and now you affect to say that you didn't intend to use it to destroy life. Were that so, why did you load it? Your language before and after the shooting at the husband and wife, showed that you intended to shoot them both'.

Concluding that 'he would be deficient in the discharge of his duty, if he didn't pass a sentence that would reflect the seriousness of the crime'. He then sentenced Thomas Doherty to 15 years penal servitude.

175

If you have enjoyed reading this book, then here are some more written by the same author and easily accessible to download onto a kindle device immediately or to buy in book form on Amazon. Some are 19th century crimes committed in Britain generally, whilst other focus on the town of Rotherham itself.

Rotherham Crime Books:

AN ALMANACK OF CRIME IN VICTORIAN ROTHERHAM

This is a grim, though true, snapshot of what life was like in the town of Rotherham during the Victorian era. Whilst many were celebrating the expansionism of the Industrial Revolution and the Empire, most people just lived their lives in the best way they could. Where better to see this than in the court cases of the time. Within these pages read about cases of women arrested wearing men's clothes, concealment of birth, more exploits of 'Rotherham Bob' and a slippery thief who managed to pawn the same wheelbarrow twice.

MYSTERY MURDER AT BOLTON-UPON-DEARNE

On 5 December 1856 two elderly people were murdered in their home, bludgeoned to death during an apparent robbery. The wounds inflicted on them were so severe, that two doctors and the Coroner stated that over many years of practice, they had never seen such violence before. Although the case was never solved at the time, new research has brought a possible killer to light. Was he the man who took the lives of these eminently respectable people? With the probable criminal, both victim's families and everyone else safely in their graves, the only person left to judge, is you.

ROCHE ABBEY MURDERS

This is the story of two deaths years apart, which was linked by a man's silver watch. By coincidence, both men were related and both were returning home to the village of Stone near Roche Abbey. Neither made it. In the first case a man was hung for the crime, although many people believed that he was innocent. Twenty three years later his nephew disappeared under strange circumstances, leaving the watch he had inherited, behind.

THE CANKLOW MURDER

On the 10 May 1880 a Rotherham man, John Henry Wood was executed at York for the murder of John Coe. The body, which was found at the side of a haystack on the Canklow Road was almost beaten to a pulp, and missing from his pockets was money and a silver watch. The victim had been on a drinking spree with Wood visiting many of the local public houses still in existence in Rotherham today, including the Stag, the Masons Arms, the Belvedere and the White Swan. The two men then ended up in a brothel on Wellgate run by a woman known as 'Big Liz'. When it became known that after the murder Wood had been seen in possession of the stolen silver watch he went on the run, and it was seven days before he was caught, tried and finally hanged. But was he the man who committed the crime?

National Crime Books:

MESSENGERS OF DEATH

It was easy to kill someone in the 19th century, much easier than it is today...

Access to arsenic could be gained for pennies and it's effects mimicked such diseases as cholera, dysentery and typhoid, all of which, at the time, were common illnesses. Other killers, such as laudanum, sulphuric acid and a rare poison called colchicum were used by the women in this book. Research proves that it was easier to kill someone by poison in rural areas than in big towns and cities. In most cases, the murder was only brought to the attention of the authorities by gossip and rumour mongering. One expert suggested that there were many hundreds of poisoning cases that remained undetected. It was said that women were more amenable to poisoning as it was a non physical type of execution. They also had less chance of detection, by travelling around the country, getting married and/or changing their name. The insidious ways in which these poisons were used, called for such women to be nicknamed 'Messengers of Death'.

Using previously unexplored cases, Margaret Drinkall reveals how women poisoners in the nineteenth century created such a culture of poisoning, that it seriously alarmed the government and the legal authorities of the time. Some women believed that spells and the power of witchcraft would protect them from the gallows. One woman offered her services as a professional poisoner, to other wives wishing to escape their husbands. Many others enjoyed the benefits of murder after insuring their relatives in burial clubs, *without the knowledge or consent* of those who were poisoned. Women in the village of Wix near Harwich used mass poisonings to rid themselves of encumbrances. As a result, local Coroners were forced to order many exhumations. This then is the story of some of those 'Messengers Of Death'...

THE OTHER WHITECHAPEL MURDER

This book deals with the true murder of Harriet Lane in 1874. She was the mistress of a middle class business man called Henry Wainwright and she disappeared on 11 September 1874. Exactly a year later to the very day, Henry asked a former employee to help him remove two parcels from his business address at 215 Whitechapel Road. The man Stokes agreed but was curious about the contents and when his former employer went for a cab he peered inside and to his horror found the chopped up remains of a woman. Following the cab Stokes managed to attract the attention of two constables and Henry was arrested with the remains. Shortly afterwards his brother was also arrested and charged with being an accomplice to the murder. This case has all the components of a typical Victorian murder, the body being transported in a cab and the body being covered in chloride of lime which was thought to destroy the remains, but in fact worked as a preservative. Using the newspapers of the period and the reports of inquests, magistrates court enquiries and the trial itself, the tale unfolds revealing many twists and turns. But what caused a frisson in the minds of the newspaper reading public was that Henry had so nearly got away with it. For a whole year the body had remained hidden and if Henry had sent Stokes for a cab instead of getting it himself, he would never have been convicted.

WOMEN ON THE GALLOWS

These are some of the cases of women who died at the end of an executioners rope for varied crimes from infanticide, murder of a grandchild and an uncle, to a woman charged with being a resurrectionist a few years after the exploits of Burke and Hare. Included are an horrific tale of a woman who took children from a workhouse and starved and beat them until some of them died. There is the case of a hard hearted stepmother who murdered her own children and her stepchildren because they were 'in the way'. Catherine Foster was so beautiful that she was called the Belle of Acton, but that didn't stop her from murdering her husband, because she never loved him and didn't want to be married. A young girl hanged for infanticide who tried to appeal to the other women lodging with her for mercy. None was shown to her and she was arrested and sentenced. All these women all ended up being hung and sometimes even these judicial deaths themselves were so horrific, that calls for the end of capital punishment was heard in Britain. Legal brains even discussed alternatives methods of execution which would hopefully be less traumatic.

ANGEL MAKERS: HOW THE VICTORIANS ENCOURAGED BABY FARMING

Almost everyone knows the name of Amelia Dyer the notorious baby farmer who was hanged in 1896. She is thought to have dispatched as many as 400 children in her career, but she was not on her own. At a time when infanticide was rife there were many more of these women operating in Britain, and the police were powerless to stop them. Only when a Society was formed which made child protection its bedrock were the activities of these woman brought to an end. It has often been suggested that in their time these women murdered thousands of innocent babies. Not for nothing were they known as Angel Makers. These are the stories of just some of them.

ARMLEY GOAL: LIFE AND DEATH IN A VICTORIAN PRISON

When Armley Gaol was built in 1847 it was intended to be one of the most modern and progressive prisons of its kind. Yet within its walls men, women and children as young as eight were kept in virtual solitary confinement for their entire sentences. Inmates were frequently given pointless hard labour punishments, such as turning the crank, and hours spent on the treadmill.

But the worst part was those prisoners found guilty of violent assaults and murder who were subject to harsh floggings, or worse still execution. Within its walls prison officers dealt with recalcitrant prisoners and inmate violence. Prison surgeons had to deal with the reality of disease and poverty, often from inmates just arriving. The prison chaplains did their best for those in their care but it is no wonder many took the chance to escape or commit suicide rather than serve out their sentences, within its walls.

Reading this account of Life and Death in Armley Gaol, will highlight some of the grisly details of prison life. In the end you will be thankful you are just visiting.

Printed in Great Britain
by Amazon